Auras

Auras

How to balance and cleanse your energy body

Hamraz Ahsan

For my darling daughter, Pawan.

Photos courtesy of Shutterstock.

© 2021 Arcturus Holdings Limited

All rights reserved. No part of this publication may be reproduced, stored in a retrieval system or transmitted in any form or by any means (including electronic, mechanical, photocopying, recording, or otherwise) without prior written permission from the publisher.

ISBN: 978-1-83940-192-3
AD008213US

Printed in China

2 4 6 8 10 9 7 5 3 1

Contents

Introduction 6

1 What are auras? 10

2 Chakras and auras 36

3 Balancing your aura 64

4 The environment and other people 94

5 Energetic protection 112

6 The Meditations 124

    Further reading 156

    Index 158

Introduction

When I wrote my novel *Kabuko the Djinn* I drew on certain meditative practices I had engaged in for several years. Those practices had, over time, enabled me to explore what the energies in a human body look and feel like. I used that knowledge to write about the invisible forces that are housed within each of us. This is the closest I could get to describing what I saw within a human being's energy body: "Such vibrant colors, so much happening all at once—light dancing, snaking, leaping, bursts of energy and rivers of light everywhere." That description attempts to introduce the reader to the dynamic and wondrous body of light that lives inside our dense physical body. It is usually not possible to see that energy body with the naked eye. However, as I hope to show you in this book, you regularly sense those energies, even if you have never seen them.

For example, have you ever met someone and taken an instant dislike to them, before they've said or done anything? Conversely, have you met someone and known within seconds that you'll get along? Have you ever entered a house and felt like it was unwelcoming, or one where you immediately felt at home and never wanted to leave? These are all examples of your energy body giving you feedback on the people you meet and the places you enter.

The idea of invisible energies has been with us since time immemorial. For example, we know that prehistoric peoples used musical instruments and their own voices in ceremonies intended to help with the uncertainties of human life. These sounds—unlike music for entertainment purposes—were designed to activate the manifestation powers of the vibrational body. Since these were preliterate societies, it's impossible to say for sure if the modern understanding of the energy body popular in spiritual circles was the same for those early people. However, in calling for help from unseen forces—be they spirits or gods—our ancestors were stepping into the realm of energy, hidden from sight but definitely there.

A devotee dances at the shrine in Lahore, Pakistan, of Sufi saint, Shah Madhu Lal Hussain. His fingers indicate that he is becoming 'one' with divine energy within the trance dance.

INTRODUCTION

The tradition I follow, that of Sufism, believes that we experience the divine when our energy body is in alignment with the vibrational force of the universe. This can be achieved by chanting the 99 names of God. It can also be achieved through dance, such as the whirling dervishes of Turkey or the *dhamal* (trance dance) practice of the devotees at Sufi shrines in the Indian subcontinent. For a person not following a particular tradition, meditation can also give rise to the same benefits of vibrational entrainment with divine energy.

In this book, you will find an understanding of your energetic structure, how to ensure that it is functioning at its optimal level, and how you can begin to understand the auras of those around you. This will help you in many practical ways in your daily life. It can ensure that you attract the best people and the best outcomes to you. It can help you decide whether you should work with a particular client, or if you should walk away from a project. When you are perfectly aligned energetically, with a clean, clear aura, you can live a life that is to your highest good.

> 'If the Milky Way were not within me, how should I have seen it or known it?'
> Kahlil Gibran

CHAPTER 1

CHAPTER 1

The history of auras

Aura means "breeze" or "breath" in the ancient Greek language, and was also the name of a lesser-known Greek Titan goddess. The word's use as a name for the part of the energy sheath (visible to some adepts) outside the physical body came into being around the end of the 19th century. This latter meaning, of a sort of halo surrounding the body, was made particularly popular in the West by the theosophists. Theosophy is a school of philosophical thought founded in the late 19th century that focuses on examining the truth of the nature of the world and spirituality. It draws on aspects of wisdom found in Hinduism, Buddhism and Western esoteric thought. The movement has so many aspects to its practice that it would take another book to fully explore it all. However, for our purposes, we should look at the work of a theosophist called Charles Webster Leadbeater.

Leadbeater wrote extensively on the makeup of the human energy body, as well as doing some very detailed sketches of his idea of what chakras (energy points) in the body look like. He drew on some ideas from the Indian subcontinent alongside his own experiences of seeing energy after having done a number of meditation practices. This work was then used as the basis of an exploration into the subject in the late 1970s by Christopher Hills. The classic seven-chakra, rainbow-colored system that you may be familiar with is the result of the work Hills did in

WHAT ARE AURAS?

that decade. We will look at two chakra systems in more detail in chapter two (pages 36–63).

Beyond the work of 19th-century theosophy luminaries, we have little historical literature on auras as we know them today. However, it has been speculated that the halos shown around the heads of religious figures in Christian iconography could be there to indicate the radiant purity of their auras. Certainly the spirit or soul has been written about extensively, and some of the ideas we have of what remains after we die can be attributed to an energy body, if not precisely to an aura.

Author W.E. Butler wrote in his work *How to Read the Aura* that: "It is said in the East that the spiritual aura of the Lord Gautama Buddha extended for two hundred miles, and they also say that the whole of this planet is held in the aura of a very great Being." Could it be that the more spiritually advanced we get, our auras become beacons of radiant joy for the world around us?

This mosaic of Christ in the arms of the Virgin Mary shows both with halos around their heads. There are those who believe that this is to show the purity of their auras.

CHAPTER 1

Everything is responsive

Huna is a life philosophy from Hawaii that has many beneficial ideas about the world around us. Serge Kahili King, a Huna practitioner, has spoken about a number of principles governing the nature of reality. Among them is one that is very important and useful to anyone interested in auras: "everything is alive and responsive." Everything has an aura, irrespective of whether it is animate or inanimate. It used to be thought likely that only living beings had an energetic aura, but many esoteric practitioners have now confirmed that all matter has an aura. If you stub your toe on a cupboard, it may well be that your aura and that of the cupboard are not in harmony, and the stubbed toe is the outcome. (Although, it may just be that you need to move the cupboard to a less inconvenient spot!)

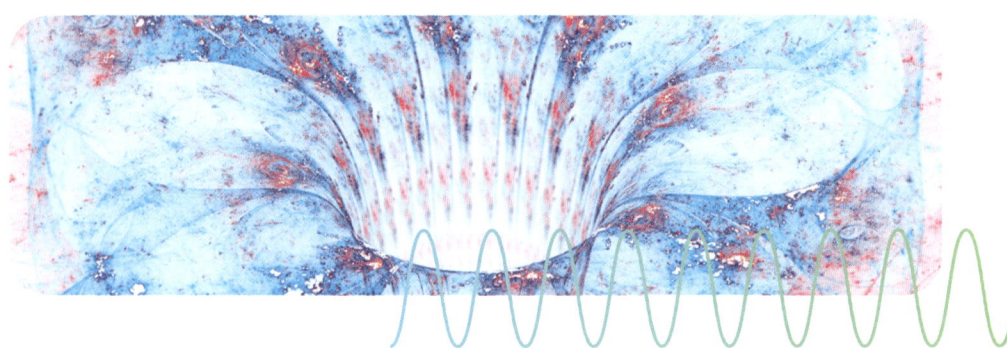

If we accept that everything has an aura, and that this aura is in constant interplay with all the other auras of things, people and places with which it interacts, then you can see how important it is to ensure that you only have around you those auras that you align well with.

PRAISE, DON'T CRITICIZE

One of the key ways in which Huna practitioners, in the tradition followed by Serge Kahili King, acknowledge the principle that everything is alive and responsive is to praise rather than criticize. This is a good way to come into harmony with all the auras of what surrounds you. A typical day might involve frustration when something doesn't work quite right. The coffee maker might not work the first time, or the shower might not get hot because the water heater isn't working properly. This might cause you to internally (or even externally) criticize and curse the inanimate objects involved and the overall quality of your life. This will immediately put you into disharmony in both your energy body and your physical experience. It is always far better to praise or to acknowledge things that do go right. How fortunate we are to have coffee makers, hot water and indoor plumbing that gives us an abundance of flowing water.

It is unrealistic to be positive all the time, even when things are going wrong, but maintaining an "attitude of gratitude" helps you to keep your auric energy clear and encourage the auras of the things and people around you to also vibrate at that higher level. You will find, over time, that life runs far more smoothly and happily.

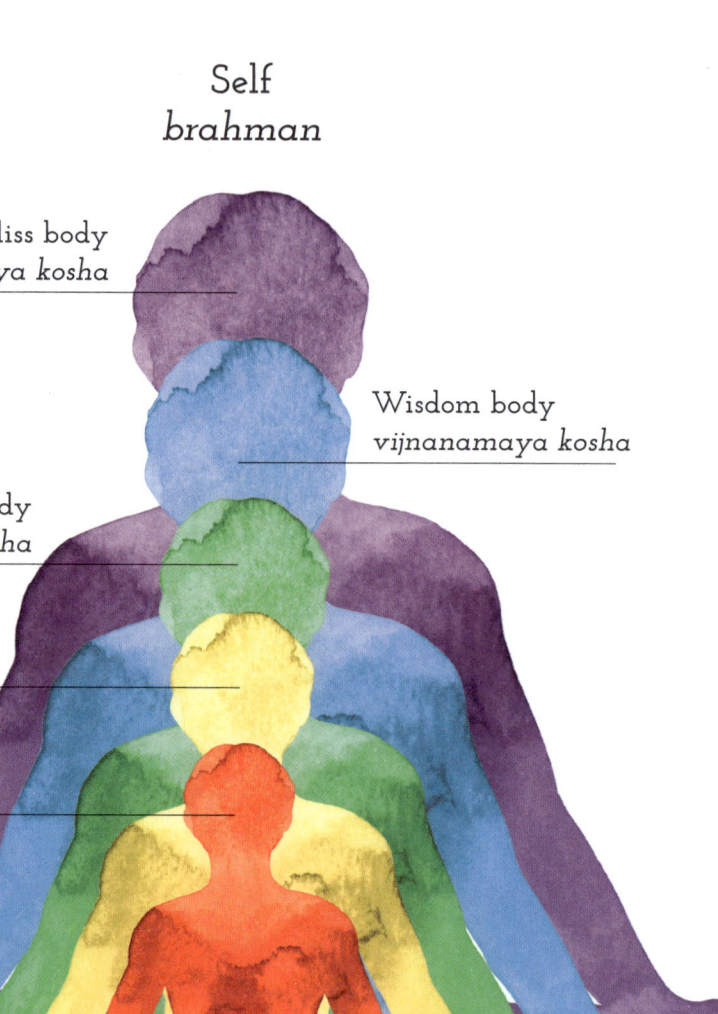

WHAT ARE AURAS?

Energetic sheaths

Different traditions believe energy is ordered in a variety of ways within the body. Some systems believe there are seven energy bodies radiating out from the skin, each concerned with a different aspect of your physical, emotional, intellectual and spiritual makeup. However, in Vedantic philosophy there are five koshas (sheaths) in the body that surround the eternal self, called the *brahman* or *atman* in the Advaita Vedanta. These sheaths each have an important role to play in keeping a person happy and healthy; they also interact with each other so that damage to one sheath will inevitably affect all the others.

You can find out more about how to restore each of the five koshas to optimum health on pages 20–24. Once you have cleared each of these five energy sheaths, you can maintain overall health by just working with one sheath, which represents all of them. If one visualizes a core, single sheath and concentrates one's efforts on keeping this clear and strong, the health of all the layers of the energy body is maintained. As such, we shall call this composite energy field the protective sheath.

THE PROTECTIVE SHEATH

The protective sheath reflects the energy of our current day-to-day life. If you could view it (and the meditation on pages 126–128 will show you how to practice doing this), you would see an ever-swirling, moving mist

CHAPTER 1

of color at the outer edge of the shape of things and people. Those changes in the energy body can happen because of your fluctuating emotions, hormonal changes, your interactions with others and your thoughts and beliefs about yourself and others.

When this sheath is working well, your intuition will be strong about situations and other people. You will see their motivations clearly and, for some, it is almost as if you have a psychic ability to know what's coming your way. That is because you do! This sheath, which has all the qualities

WHAT ARE AURAS?

of the koshas, affects your psychic abilities keenly, and working to keep it clear and healthy is a good way to stay psychically alert.

If this sheath is damaged or weak, you can be left open to psychic attack. This is when you begin to attract unwelcome experiences to you, and life begins to have an increasing level of frustration to it. By working to strengthen this sheath, you can ensure you only attract those experiences to you that work for your highest good and make you feel positive and blissful about life.

CHAPTER 1

CLEANSING THE ANNAMAYA KOSHA

The annamaya kosha is also known as the physical body, or the food sheath. This is because it is your physical self, which comprises what you eat and this corporeal body, that will become food for the Earth and its creatures, once your *atman,* or soul, has left this plane of existence.

It is therefore natural that the best way to cleanse and protect this part of your energetic makeup is good nutrition and maintaining excellent physical health. You may think that the physical is not as important as the spiritual when it comes to auras, but this is not true. You reside in your body, and any discomfort here will affect all your energy sheaths.

While it is beyond the scope of this book to advise on diet, it would be beneficial to look into booking an ayurvedic session to understand your specific body type and which foods will support your overall physical health. As a general rule of thumb for everyone, avoiding processed foods and veering toward whole, organically produced foods is best.

You can also cleanse this part of your auric body through exercise. However, be aware that the third leg of the tripod of physical health is relaxation, so do not undertake overly strenuous exercise. You can find some helpful yoga *asanas* to do on pages 70–87.

CLEANSING THE PRANAMAYA KOSHA

Pranamaya is the kosha that pertains to energy, since *prana* means energy. It is the vital energy that courses through the meridians or *nadis* of your body. This energy intersects at certain points called chakras, which we will learn more about in the next chapter (see pages 36–63).

If this energy sheath is not operating at full health, you will suffer from breathing problems and may lose your sense of smell or experience chronic fatigue. Working with the breath is the best way to cleanse this kosha. A daily breathing practice is recommended for all people as being as necessary as brushing your teeth in the morning.

You can do the alternate nostril breathing exercise on pages 72–73 as a quick and easy way to bring this sheath into alignment. Not only does this exercise restore the workings of this kosha, it also balances the "male" and "female" energies in the body, so you physically experience equilibrium. It does not matter what sex or gender you are, or how you identify yourself at all, as this is a cosmic duality at play that resides in all matter, irrespective of how it is presented biologically—we all have masculine and feminine energy as a dual experience within us which is usually resolved into one at the point of death or enlightenment.

CHAPTER 1

CLEANSING THE MANOMAYA KOSHA

Have you ever heard the saying "energy flows to where attention goes"? This sheath, which is often called the mental or the emotional body kosha, shows the truth of that saying. Your emotions (the "energy" part of the saying) arise from your thoughts (the "attention" part of the saying), and those emotions have a direct influence on your health. Medical researchers have found that those with a positive outlook on life and optimistic thoughts live longer, healthier lives than those who are negative and pessimistic. So one of the best ways to cleanse and protect this sheath is to think good thoughts. Think well of people and, as seen on page 15, praise and don't criticise the world around you.

Another way to heal this sheath is to do anything that stops you from overthinking, so meditation, chanting and restorative yoga poses are all good for this. Since the way we think is often formed in childhood, it is very good to do the yoga *asana* Child's Pose (see pages 84–85). This helps us stop dwelling on, and feeling emotionally hurt by, thoughts of conflict or injustice. If you can put aside ideas that are causing you pain, you will heal this body and send vibrations of joy throughout your whole energy system.

CLEANSING THE VIJNANAMAYA KOSHA

This is where your intuition, wisdom and inspiration reside. Damage to this kosha will cause you to doubt yourself, feel unconnected to your spiritual truth, and give rise to depression and despair.

Mindfulness can help heal this sheath, since we are going beyond the world of rationality to a place of being the timeless "witness." This is the eternal part of yourself, the Buddha mind, that observes without judgment or attachment.

If you find that meditation or mindfulness does not work for you, you could try more traditional talking therapies to resolve problems in your Manomaya kosha, which will then affect the Vijnanamaya. The important thing is to go beyond the physical and to your own sense of spiritual awareness. This is the case even on a secular level, as you do not need to follow any religious or spiritual tradition to understand that energy is more than what we see in the material world. Take a quantum physics class if you really want to get a scientific understanding of what spiritual traditions have been saying about energy for millennia.

CHAPTER 1

CONNECTING TO THE ANANDAMAYA KOSHA

This is called the Bliss body because when you understand experientially that we are all one connected energy manifesting in different forms, that realization is a blissful feeling. You may have felt this sensation when you are in a state of complete absorption in what you are doing, as described by psychologist Mihaly Csikszentmihalyi in his groundbreaking book *Flow*. You experience complete connection to what you are doing, and your thoughts and the ego are no longer calling the shots. You can also experience this feeling spontaneously through meditation practices. It takes time and practice to get to that feeling, but it is achievable and, once experienced, it becomes easier to tap back into it.

You do not really "cleanse" or heal this kosha, because it is always perfect. But problems in other sheaths can cause the connection between this part of our energy body to become disconnected from the rest. You can reconnect by doing charitable works that permit you to see that the people you are helping are no different from you. Once we understand *spiritually*, rather than intellectually, that we are all one, we connect to the bliss of this kosha.

Cleansing the protective sheath

Once you have thought about cleansing and connecting with your five koshas, you can simply maintain your energetic health by concentrating your efforts on the sum of those sheaths and visualizing it as a single protective sheath. There are several ways to cleanse this sheath. I recommend you do at least one a day and, ideally, create a monthly routine that incorporates all the suggestions below.

SMUDGING

Burning bundles of dried herbs is a tried-and-tested way to clear not just your own aura but the aura of the space around you. This is because your senses are a great conduit to your energy body. The scent of the herbs burning helps you feel transported to a more spiritual space in which you can visualize healing your body—both physical and energetic.

You can buy ready-made smudging sticks in alternative health shops, or you can make your own with bundles of dried herbs. Just make sure you have a fireproof dish available to catch any stray embers. Light the bundle, blow it out so that the end is smoking, and pass whatever you're smudging

CHAPTER 1

through the fragrant smoke. You can smudge your own aura by starting at your feet and moving the smoke up the left-hand side of your body, over the top of your head and down your right-hand side. Once you've finished, make sure you extinguish the smudgestick completely.

Herbs to smudge with:
- sage
- thyme
- rosemary
- cedar
- mugwort

SALT BATHS

Salt has long been considered a sacred substance—the taste of our tears, our bodies, the sea and the earth. Salt is also immensely cleansing and can be used to cleanse an aura easily and quickly. Whenever you feel particularly down or tired, simply take a couple of handfuls of one of the salts below and add them to a warm bath. When sitting in the bath, visualize the saltwater  sparkling with a cleansing light, and be sure to pass the water over your head and rub some of it on your belly button.

Salts to use:
❖ Epsom salt (this is not a salt in the sense of the others listed, but has many additional health benefits)
❖ Sea salt
❖ Himalayan pink salt
❖ Rosemary-infused salts
❖ Black salt (also called Kala Namak)

CHANTING

The right sounds can be very cleansing to your aura, especially when the sounds are reverberating through your body. As we will see in chapter two (pages 36–63), there are sounds connected to cleansing each chakra in the seven-chakra system, but there are also chants you can do that relate to a general aura cleansing without reference to a specific chakra. Try *Aah-Ummn* as a chant, opening your mouth like an O initially and then closing it and feeling the hum of the last part of the sound against your lips. Always prepare for your chant sessions by bathing, sitting in a clean room and, perhaps, lighting some incense if you like the smell of it. If you begin to feel light-headed, stop chanting, stamp your feet on the ground and rub your palms against your thighs. Chanting suits some people, but not everyone. So if you find you get headaches, earaches or feel dizzy after chanting, choose another method of aura cleansing.

DRINK WATER

This may sound like a ridiculous suggestion, but one way in which your aura will weaken considerably is if you are not adequately hydrated. Your physical body impacts your aura, which is why certain clairvoyants can "see" illnesses in a person's aura. When you are physically healthy, you have a far greater chance of keeping your aura clear and balanced. So drink at least eight glasses of water a day and remember that you will need more on hotter days when you sweat out a lot of water.

BODY MASSAGE

One of the most enjoyable ways of clearing your aura is massage with appropriate oils. You can ask a partner or family member to give you a massage or you can massage yourself. One of the best areas to massage is your feet. This is because they connect you to the earth and are a key area for strengthening your aura. After washing them, anoint them with oil and massage from the heel up to the toes—and remember to massage between your toes as well. Be careful if you're doing this on a slippery surface, and perhaps put socks on immediately afterwards to allow the oil to sink into your feet. If you're using essential oils, make sure you use a base oil, such as almond or coconut, so that you're not applying strong oils straight onto your skin.

CHAPTER 1

Oils to use:
- ❖ rose oil to feel loved and supported
- ❖ basil oil to attract prosperity
- ❖ lavender oil to de-stress
- ❖ rosemary oil to promote healing
- ❖ bergamot oil to energize yourself

A CALM DEMEANOR

Try to avoid outrage, whether online or in conversation. Outrage, conflict and anger cause your aura to weaken. Dr Andrew Weil, a practitioner of integrative medicine, suggested in one of his early books on optimum health that everyone take regular "news fasts" so we don't take on negativity. This is even more useful for social media. If you don't know what the latest outrage is, you can't fall prey to its effects. Anger and counter-anger can be a very destructive cycle, and nobody—unless they have an abnormal energy exchange that I would not consider beneficial or helpful—feels better after an argument.

WALK BAREFOOT

Connecting with the earth heals you both physically and psychically. If you can manage it, regularly walk barefoot on the earth. This is a process called "earthing," and it ensures that your body clock is calibrated to the pulse of the Earth. It connects you with your own nature and relieves you from the stress of electromagnetic waves that constantly affect our auras.

MEDITATION

In chapter six (pages 124–155) you can find a range of different meditations that you can do to work with your aura and that of others. However, a regular meditation practice, even if you're not trying to do anything in particular, is extremely beneficial. There are now several apps that can help you take a little time each day to relax. You can also take a class if you think it's too difficult to learn to meditate by yourself. Even a few moments relaxing and trying not to think about anything in particular can help you during a busy day.

CHAPTER 1

Seeing the aura

Semyon Davidovich Kirlian invented Kirlian photography in 1939, a process by which he was able to photograph the aura around living things. In 1961, Kirlian and his journalist wife, Valentina, published an article on the subject in the *Russian Journal of Scientific and Applied*

WHAT ARE AURAS?

Photography. Ever since that time, researchers and energy healers have used the information gained through Kirlian photography to diagnose illnesses and predict the preoccupations of the people being photographed.

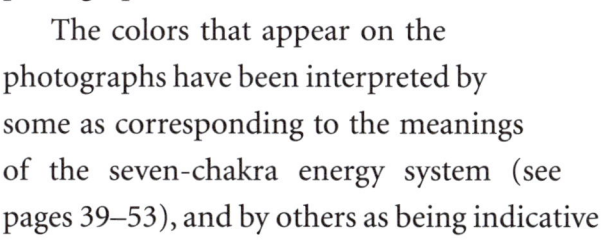

The colors that appear on the photographs have been interpreted by some as corresponding to the meanings of the seven-chakra energy system (see pages 39–53), and by others as being indicative of certain personality traits and of what concerns the person has at the time of being photographed. Kirlian's work has definitely increased the interest in auras, but there was another earlier practitioner who invented a way for people to see the aura with the naked eye.

KILNER SCREENS

Dr W.J. Kilner wrote in his 1911 book *The Human Atmosphere* about investigations he made into the human aura by virtue of his colored screens. The screens are made of thin glass with dicyanin dyes in alcohol. The operator looks through a dark screen at the light screens for a minute or so, and then looks at the person being read through a pale

CHAPTER 1

screen until he or she can see the aura. Regular use of the screens results in the operator eventually being able to see auras without the aid of any apparatus. Much like Magic Eye pictures, popular in student culture in the 1990s, once you have adjusted your eye to perceive the aura, it's hard to go back. A plain black or white background behind the subject is required, but looking at the aura in this way can cause pain in the eyes, so should be undertaken with care.

Theosophist Arthur E. Powell described what the aura, seen in this way, looks like in his book *The Etheric Double*: "The Inner Aura is the densest portion of the aura proper. It is usually more distinctly marked and broader in persons in robust physical health. The Outer Aura commences from the outer edge of the Inner Aura and, unlike the Inner Aura, varies in size considerably. Round the head it extends usually about 2 inches beyond the shoulders: by the sides and body of the trunk, it is a little narrower. It follows closely the contours of the body, being sometimes a little narrower down the lower limbs. Around the arms it corresponds to that encircling the legs, but is generally broader round the hands and frequently projects a long distance from the finger tips."

This last part of the description pertaining to the hands will be important for us later when we look at how to balance our auras through our hands (see pages 88–90).

PSYCHIC SIGHT

Despite these more technical ways to see the aura, the most popular among practitioners remains the gift of psychically viewing the aura. This may not necessarily be a visual impression, and it may be that it is "viewed" through feelings and emotions that the healer gets as they sit across from you, in the influence of your aura. Some may even use the flat of the palm to "feel" the edges of the aura by placing their hand a couple of inches away from the body.

If you would like to develop such a sight, you should take care to ensure that you keep your protective sheath in top condition, as you will only be able to get clear impressions of the auras of others if your own is strong and healthy. Otherwise, you may sense gaps in their aura when it is actually a problem with your own. You can find a variety of ways to cleanse your protective sheath on pages 25–31.

Chakras and auras

The Chakras

Chakras are energy points within the body that act as whirlpools that help distribute energy (called *prana* in Ayurveda and *chi* in Traditional Chinese Medicine) properly inside the body. A blocked chakra can cause problems in the aspect of life that relates to that particular chakra. So, for example, in the seven-chakra system (see below), the heart chakra relates to relationships, and a blockage here will make it hard to attract and maintain loving relationships. It is important to keep your chakras working well, as this will also have an impact on your aura.

THE SEVEN-CHAKRA SYSTEM

Most people would assume that the colorful seven-chakra system that many yogis are familiar with originates in ancient Indian writings—and indeed the Upanishads (800 BCE – 400 BCE) do mention seven chakras. But there is no mention of colors, and many of the healing modalities used in the West would not be recognized by scholars of ancient Indian scriptures. Our modern understanding of the seven-chakra system actually owes more to writers in the 1970s in the West than to the Vedic writings. Since that time, practitioners around the world have accepted the colors given at that time for the seven chakras. However, the mantras associated with them have their root in Vedic writings, where chanting is used to raise energy up the spine from the root to the crown chakra in order to gain spiritual advancement.

CHAPTER 2

MULADHARA THE ROOT CHAKRA

❖ **Color**: Red
❖ **Mantra**: Laam

The location of this chakra is at the base of the spine, at the point of your pelvic floor. This energy point relates to our basic needs, such as food, shelter, sleep and safety. It is the foundation upon which we are built. If you have weakness or problems in your energy at this chakra, you will find it difficult to trust people and will suffer from a lack of security in your life. You may have nightmares or problems with your lower limbs, and it can result in prostate issues in men. Loss of smell and eating disorders are also indications of problems here.

Interestingly, it used to be rare to find Muladhara problems in people in the developing world. This is counterintuitive, as you would think parts of the world where life is precarious and one's basic needs may not be met would have more root-chakra issues. However, a clue may be found in the fact that traditionally people were far more likely to squat, sitting on the floor rather than on a chair. Even now, one of the ways in which we can bring this chakra back

into alignment is to squat more, whether in *Malasana* (squatting) yogic poses or simply sitting in a squat when at rest.

If squatting is difficult or indeed impossible for you, you can also help balance this chakra through chanting. The mantra for this chakra is laam. The sound is almost "laarm," but as you begin to chant it, you will begin to settle into the sound in a way that feels right to you.

Before you undertake any chakra-clearing work, remember to bathe and put a specific time aside each week to do your chanting. You are trying to impress upon your subconscious that you are about to undertake energetic work.

If you have fears around money and how you will be provided for in the future, returning this chakra to optimum operation will help you let go of those worries. You will find that this first chakra is where you awaken your energy, and it will begin your journey to energetic health. Oddly enough, many strange and wonderful coincidences and events begin to manifest when you begin the work of awakening the kundalini energy that lives here, at the base of your spine. It is very powerful work and should be undertaken by everyone who wishes to live the very best life possible physically, mentally, emotionally and spiritually.

CHAPTER 2

SVADHISTHANA THE SACRAL CHAKRA

- ❖ **Color:** Orange
- ❖ **Mantra:** Vaam

The location of this chakra is just above the pubic bone and below the navel. Its position is appropriate, as it relates to sexuality as well as creativity. Creativity used to mean the very literal act of creating a child, but in the modern world, this can be about creating a work of art, a home you love, or a relationship that is nurturing and special. You can define what it is that you create.

An imbalance here can result in sexual dysfunction, frustrated creative endeavors, and becoming humorless and sullen. Instead of fearing failure when embarking on any creative endeavor such as painting a picture or learning a dance, embrace it as a natural and enjoyable part of the experience. Laugh if you feel you haven't achieved what you want to because, in truth, all of life is simply play, with an illusion of importance or reality superimposed upon it.

You can do left-nostril breathing as a way to balance this chakra. Close your right nostril with the index and middle fingers of your right hand

and breathe gently 10 times through your left nostril. This increases the feminine energy in your body and is congruent with this chakra's energy makeup. If you feel you have the symptoms of a second-chakra problem, you can do this for seven days before returning to your usual morning breathing practice. Do not do it in conjunction with the alternate-nostril breathing we explore on pages 72–73.

Chanting is another way to balance the chakras. The mantra for this one is vaam, pronounced "vaarm." If you feel that the last sound is extending some way as you chant it, this is fine. Your body has an intuitive knowledge about which sounds you can produce for your healing, so go with it unless you are chanting in a guided group. Chanting in groups is quite different from chanting alone, as you are blending your aura with the auras of everyone else in your group and you must try not to introduce a discordant element into the group chant.

Remember, as always, to instigate a sense of ritual when you sit to chant or do any energy work. Your subconscious must be impressed with the idea that this is a special time in order to properly effect an energetic shift. You can inject your work with ritual by ensuring you do your practices at a particular time of day, in a specific room, or wearing a specific outfit just for energy work. Peace silk (silk extracted without killing silk worms) is particularly good for this purpose, but you can wear any natural, ethically sourced clothes when doing energy work. You then subconsciously know it's time for energy work when you put on those clothes and enter that room at that specific time.

CHAPTER 2

MANIPURA
THE SOLAR PLEXUS CHAKRA

❖ **Color**: Yellow
❖ **Mantra**: Raam

This chakra, located at your solar plexus, just above the navel and below the rib cage, is vitally important for the modern world. That's because this is where the intellect lies, and we often sacrifice the spiritual for the intellectual in modern life. This is also the seat of your personal power and your individual will. It is the chakra that will show you if it is imbalanced in directly observable ways. Digestive problems and loss of confidence are just two problems associated with this chakra. Low self-esteem, lack of self-control and anger-management issues are others.

One way you can bring this chakra into balance is through the exercises given relating to the Naaf on pages 67–69. You can also help heal this chakra by doing the Warrior *asana* on pages 80–81.

This is one of the few energy centers that you can work with on a purely intellectual level by writing out your goals and desires in a journal. If you achieve clarity about where you want to go intellectually, you can use chanting and other energetic practices to manifest those goals and reassure your energy body that you have retained your personal power. It is important for the good functioning of this chakra that you ensure you have expressed your individual will through appropriate maturation and a healthy relationship with your parents. If your relationship with your parents is dysfunctional, consider a class in counseling or another healing therapy in order to resolve it.

The chant for this chakra is raam, which is pronounced as it is written. Try and ensure that you engage your diaphragm by placing your hand on your belly and allowing your breath to go out fully with each chant.

You can also resolve any problems here through diet and intermittent fasting. Please always consult a medical professional before undertaking a fast or considering a change in diet, especially if you are on medication. You can discover your body type, or *dosha*, by booking an Ayurvedic session, which will provide advice on what would be most energetically beneficial for you to eat and drink. Even though it is based on different principles and knowledge, Traditional Chinese Medicine also works very well for digestive problems that arise from a blockage in this chakra. TCM shares the view that the food and drinks we consume affect us energetically, and advice is given on how to come back into equilibrium through a change in nutrition.

CHAPTER 2

ANAHATA THE HEART CHAKRA

- ❖ **Color:** Green
- ❖ **Mantra:** yaam

This chakra is located in the middle of the chest, and is where compassion, love and kindness live. It is vitally important for maintaining good relationships, not just romantically, but also with everyone you come into contact with.

An imbalance here will stop you from feeling loved or being able to give love. The unconditional nature of the love you should give is hinted at in the meaning of the Sanskrit word Anahata; it means "unhurt." In relationships, we are often hurt because we see ourselves as separate from the person we love. If we are concerned with being right over being kind, we will never experience true love.

It is said that a mother's love is the only true love; you may have a hard time believing this if you have an unhappy or abusive relationship with your mother, but it alludes to the fact that, when pregnant, a mother is so intrinsically linked to her baby that what she eats, drinks and feels are felt by her baby through her digestive, respiratory, cardiovascular and hormonal systems. What happens to one happens to the other. This is what true love is: an empathy and sharing of experience so deep that you lose yourself in it. If you are to connect with others in a loving manner, this chakra must be functioning well.

The first way to heal this chakra is by showing self-love. Stop the internal criticism and never speak ill of yourself. Your body and spirit hear everything you say, and calling yourself stupid or clumsy or any of the other negative words we might use is extremely harmful. Buy yourself flowers. Light fragrant candles. Woo yourself and eat dinner for one on your best porcelain plates. Self-care must be a priority, because only when you love yourself can you overflow with love for others.

The chant for this chakra is yaam, and can be pronounced "yum." Imagine as you chant that you are sending out love to all beings in the universe. You can visualize this love as a rose-colored, sparkling energy making its way out of your chest, through your mouth, out into the world and infusing everything with light and joy.

Remember to take that feeling of love and healing into the world outside your meditation room. It's all very well to meditate on love and attempt to clear your heart chakra; but if you're not walking the chant in your everyday life, you will remain blocked here. Smile more. Allow people to cut in front of you in line. Treat everyone as if they were a most beloved part of you.

CHAPTER 2

VISUDDHA THE THROAT CHAKRA

- ❖ **Color:** Blue
- ❖ **Mantra:** Haam

This chakra is located just above your collarbone at the base of your throat, and is the communication center. This is the first of the higher spiritual chakras, and it is most in alignment when you're speaking your truth. This means that you have properly and fully expressed what it is that you hold in your heart.

We often say things to please others; we may agree to do more work for the boss when we know we need a break, or say we'd love to see friends when we'd rather stay at home watching movies and eating ice cream. We may tell someone we'll go on a second date out of guilt rather than because we really want to. This way a blocked throat chakra and an unhappy aura lies.

Do you often get a sore throat? Do you regularly lose your voice? These are both signs that your throat chakra is blocked. A simple way to remedy this immediately is to look at your schedule and see what you have coming up. Is there anything you don't want to do, but are doing out of obligation? Cancel it. Obviously, not everything can be dealt with in this way; you may have a funeral you have to attend, or a sibling's wedding. This is not an excuse to jettison every responsibility you have; but you can definitely think more deeply about what you have agreed to do and excise the things you don't want from your life.

Have you ever had an experience where you've agreed to do something you don't want to do, but then you get sick, so you can't do it anyway? This is because your body will kick into action to respond to whatever you tell it on an energetic level, even if your calendar says something different.

To facilitate better communication, you can wear a blue scarf or necktie for a while. However, chanting works best for this chakra, because sound is its power. The chant for this chakra is haam, and it is pronounced "harm." Open your mouth fairly wide when chanting for this chakra, as you are encouraging yourself to speak up.

You will know yourself which areas in your life require you to speak more truthfully. However, this is not to suggest that you be unkind in anything you say. Remember the golden rule, often attributed to the Sufi poet Rumi: "Before you speak, let your words pass through three gates. At the first gate ask yourself, 'Is it true?' At the second gate ask, 'Is it necessary?' At the third gate ask, 'Is it kind?'"

CHAPTER 2

AJNA
THE THIRD EYE CHAKRA

❖ **Color**: Indigo
❖ **Mantra**: Aum

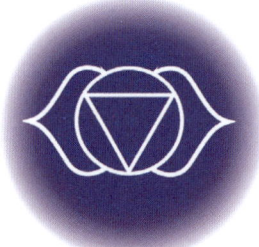

This chakra is located in the middle of the forehead, between the eyebrows, and is the seat of intuition and a connection to divine consciousness. If you are keen to see auras and develop other psychic skills, this energy center must be working well and in proper alignment. Much like the Vijnanamaya kosha (see page 23), any imbalance here will show up as a disconnection from your intuition and sixth sense.

The Child's Pose (see pages 84–85) is a good yoga *asana* to do to help bring this chakra back into alignment. The *asana* is named well, because our intuition is strongest when we are children and, as we grow into adults, for the sake of society we suppress many of our natural abilities. In Child's Pose, you place your forehead gently on the yoga mat and connect with the earth. This is very healing.

When my step-grandchildren were very young, my son-in-law would gently stroke the place of the third eye between their eyebrows until they fell asleep. Try it yourself with a partner and you will find it very soothing. When we are alert in the day, our intuition is working overtime to keep us safe, so this act relaxes us from alert mode into relaxation mode.

The chant for this chakra is aum and it is pronounced "aa–uu–eemm." This is sometimes written as om, but the pronunciation is better as aum. It is a very powerful chant, and a regular practice with this sound will result in the opening of this high spiritual chakra. People report being able to see auras very easily when they are working with this energy center.

You can also help the working of this chakra by anointing it regularly with a suitable oil after you wash your face in the morning. Jasmine is an oil I use for this purpose, but oils from most night-blooming flowers will work just as well. Avoid rose in anointing this part of the body, as its energy is more suited to the opening of the lower chakras.

You may find that this energy center becomes clear without you needing to do any work on it at all, once you have finished working with the koshas, your protective sheath and the lower chakras. The effect of energy work is cumulative, and works from the physical upwards. So a strong, healthy body with good thoughts, emotions and actions will result in good intuition and higher powers of wisdom and insight.

CHAPTER 2

SAHASRARA THE CROWN CHAKRA

- ❖ **Color:** Violet
- ❖ **Mantra:** None—silent contemplation

This chakra is located at the top of your head, and is the point where we connect to universal energy. If any of your lower chakras are blocked, it will be hard for you to feel the full functioning of this chakra and enjoy the fruits of divine guidance.

It is neither necessary nor advisable to concentrate on opening or unblocking this particular chakra, as it is a gift that we all have when our energy body is working well. It is far better to work on clearing all other chakras and aspects of your energy body. Once this is done, you can establish a meditation practice that includes asking for divine guidance.

You do not have to follow a particular religion or spiritual tradition to enjoy a connection with universal energy. We are beings of light, and our intuition, love and wisdom prove that we are more than just the sum of our flesh and bones.

CHAPTER 2

Colors and their meanings

Most chakra systems use color, but be aware that when you begin working with your energy body, the colors you see (or get an impression of, psychically) may not tally with those of established chakra systems. Don't worry too much about what a color is supposed to mean; concentrate more on what something feels like to you.

For example, the color for the crown chakra in the seven-chakra system is violet, while in the Sufi chakra system, it is an iridescent, shining black. Both are valid, as is whatever you see when you begin to do exercises to view the energy body.

The author Joseph Ostrom has speculated that it may well be that human sight and the colors we are able to see has evolved over the years. "There is some evidence that modern human beings see a larger variety of colors than their ancestors. Homer has described the Aegean Sea as being 'wine-dark'—a dark red? In my travel to the Greek Islands, I have spent a lot of time looking at the sea; believe me, it's a very beautiful light blue-green. It is said that Aristotle saw only reds, greens and yellows. Were the Greeks color-blind? It seems unlikely. Those who are usually have difficulty seeing reds, not blues. The perception of blues seems to be a more recent development for human beings." As such, an obsession with what each color means is not as important as what each color "feels like" to us when we look at it.

- Point of mantle
- Point of veiled
- Point of mystery
- Point of soul
- Point of heart
- Point of carnal self

The chakras in Sufism

There are six chakras, or *lataif*, in Sufism. The Sufi chakras can be activated through trance dance or *dhikr*, Islamic devotional chanting. Different Sufi traditions attribute different colors and attributes to the energy points in the body. Some only have five points, and there are some who believe that the number of energy centers in the body is infinite since we reflect the universe within ourselves. However, all agree that the *lataif* sit mostly horizontally, across the body, rather than in the vertical formation of the more familiar seven-chakra system. Some Sufi orders do not engage in dance or music, and believe in silent rather than vocal *dhikr*.

All these differences should encourage you because, as you progress through your journey into discovering more about your own aura, you will see what feels most true to you about your energy centers. The most important thing is to trust your intuition. We are somewhat enthralled by facts, figures and science-speak in the West, but energy often uses the ethereal, the intuitive and the mysterious to bring us its best gifts. Stay alert and aware, but also trust yourself if you have a particular sense of your energy.

CHAPTER 2

POINT OF CARNAL SELF

- ❖ **Color:** Yellow
- ❖ **Position:** Its center is in the solar plexus

This is the chakra that pertains to the body and material existence. The body is sacred because it houses your spirit, but in order to fully move forward to the completion of your energetic destiny, you must transcend this *lataifa* (the singular term for chakra).

One of the best ways to do this is to anchor your practice in the body through *dhamal.* **Dhamal** is a Sufi trance dance, and you can obtain drumming tapes that enable you to enter into this state. It is a form of transcendence that shares much with shamanic journeying in that you lose your everyday consciousness in order to commune with the Divine. Initially, you move in rhythm to the beat, but there are no set movements; it is based purely on sensation and how the energy of the drums moves you. It is said that, once in a trance, you become a puppet with strings of energy connecting you to God, and you move whichever way your Maker wants. It is a magical way to clear your first chakra, and you will find that your body may well miraculously heal itself of any number of ailments as a result.

POINT OF HEART

- ❖ **Color:** Red
- ❖ **Position:** Its center is an inch or so below the left breast

Sufism is often called the ancient wisdom of the heart, so this point is an important one. It is often through the remembrance of love (and, as we saw when looking at the Anahata chakra on pages 46–47, true love is unconditional) that transcendence is achieved. Ultimate union with the Beloved occurs through the opening of the heart.

Having left the Point of the Carnal Self behind in your energy work, here you begin to meditate on the nature of the Divine and the fact that your soul will return to the source of all creation.

When you are in meditation, you may find that naturally, over time, you feel a warmth in your chest and a sensation of release as this *lataifa* is activated. You will feel an outpouring of love and compassion for all and, ultimately, an understanding of your true nature as a spark of divine energy made manifest for a short time only before returning home to its source.

CHAPTER 2

POINT OF SOUL

- **Color:** White
- **Position:** Its center is an inch or so below the right breast

The progression of activation of the Sufi chakras is best undertaken with a teacher. For example, chanting is based on the teachings of your tradition, and the correct chant for each *lataifa* is given to the seeker in that setting.

However, it can be revealed that many believe all *lataif* are aspects of the heart, since this is the energy center through which we gain union with the Divine. One of the ways in which you can progress from the dhamal activation of the Point of the Carnal and meditation to open the heart is to undertake gazing at this stage of your journey. There are many ways of gazing and, when you begin to see the auras of people and things, you will become very adept at gazing. Sufis use gazing at one's teacher, or into a mirror, to help unlock the truth in their hearts. You can also do so through *sagale-naseer*, the practice of gazing at the tip of one's nose. This is done when seated in meditation, having done your usual ablutions beforehand.

POINT OF MYSTERY

- ❖ **Color**: Green
- ❖ **Position**: It is situated between the points of heart and soul in the middle of chest

The nature of this *lataifa* is revealed at the correct time for the seeker. Purity is an important concept for all those who would attain the activation of this chakra. We think of purity as simply a function of cleanliness, but this does not just pertain to one's physical body or environment. You can have someone who is physically very clean residing in a tidy, immaculate place, but if they have hate in their heart, the whole energy of the person and place is polluted.

To be pure is to be kind and loving, and to remember the sacred nature of all things since we are all one. We saw earlier that your thoughts matter, so when you feel anger or irritation, stop, breathe and remember to send loving thoughts to whoever has caused you that tension. Only then will the Point of Mystery be open to you and enable you to progress on your journey to enlightenment and union with the Divine.

CHAPTER 2

POINT OF VEILED

- ❖ **Color**: Dark blue
- ❖ **Position**: It is situated in the middle of the forehead, popularly known as the third eye

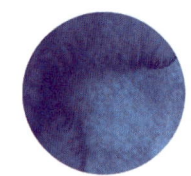

This is the first of the two higher *lataif*, and is the meeting point between the soul (spirit) and the body. Everything from the Divine comes to this point and is then distributed to other points. This is why whenever you see someone attaining enlightenment in the movies, their third eye is shown as being open or having a light radiating from it.

This chakra will only open and activate once the others are clear and functioning properly. This is because you must be able to handle the energies that come into your body at this stage. Often, problems occur when people are greedy for union with the Divine but they ignore the correct progression of energetic evolution. You wouldn't enter a toddler who didn't yet know how to walk properly into a marathon and expect them to complete it. In much the same way, spiritually you must learn to walk before you can run. Everything happens at the right time, so stay the course and clear your energies in preparation for when enlightenment will find you.

POINT OF MANTLE

- ❖ **Color**: Shining, iridescent black
- ❖ **Position**: It is situated in the crown of the head

The mantle is a cloak that envelopes you, and this point is a center of protection. When a parent puts a loving hand on the head of a child, you get the spiritual energy of this *lataifa*. The Divine puts a hand lovingly on our heads at the Point of Mantle. We honor that loving energy by ensuring that we are a worthy recipient of it.

The responsibility we all bear for ourselves culminates at this point. Living with love in our hearts and following good energetic practices will ensure that your energy body is a pure vehicle to be crowned with  this point. However, this second higher *lataifa* does not require any specific practice for its good functioning. Even if we do not activate the other *lataif*, this one is there for the protection of our eternal souls, which are not concerned with the details of our mundane existence. This can be a very cheering thought if you have problems with any of your other chakras, as nobody is ever closed off to the workings of grace.

CHAPTER 3

Balancing your aura

CHAPTER 3

Physical balance

There is a strong link between your physical body and your aura. Your thoughts affect your physical body and your physical body affects your spiritual one. The three interact constantly, and good health and wellbeing rely on each aspect being well-balanced. It is always a good idea to begin with the physical, as it is the foundation upon which your energetic health is based.

The Naaf

Naaf is a Persian word that means belly button. In the connection between the physical and the spiritual, your belly button is vitally important, and your gut is an organ to which you should pay plenty of attention. The navel is the seat of power in many occult traditions. Swami Brahmavidya wrote in *The Science of Self Knowledge* (1922): "Another great key I will give you is to be found by the contemplation of the Manipur Lotus, which is in the navel, or thereabouts. By contemplating this center, you will be able to enter and go into another person's body, take possession of that person's mind, and cause him to think and to do what you want him to do; you will obtain the power of transmuting metals, of healing the sick and afflicted, and of seership." While no moral modern person wants to take possession of another's mind, healing the sick and obtaining seership would be handy traits to have.

The word "navel" has its root in an old Anglo-Saxon word: *nafela*. The Greek word for navel is *bembix*, which literally means "whirlpool," hinting at how the movement of chakras has been described by almost all energetic medicine practitioners. Most interestingly of all, the root word for "umbilical" in Latin is *umbo*, which means the boss of a shield—the rounded, strongest part of a shield. This is a good indication of how far our strength lies in this part of our bodies.

It is not just the human body that has this center of energy; many believe there are places on Earth that serve the same function in physical geography. In Abrahamic religions, Jerusalem is considered the navel of the world. Cuzco, an important city in Peru, is named for the Quechua (Inca) word for navel. The axis mundi (or center of the Earth) is said to be the place of connection between Heaven and Earth. For the Sioux it is the Black Hills, in the Great Plains of North America. Likewise, Mount Fuji is the axis mundi of Japan. You can read more about places of power on pages 102–106.

NAVEL-GAZING

The term "navel-gazing" is often used in a disparaging way to suggest someone who is far too interested in themselves or in a particular issue to look up and see the bigger picture. However, it actually derives from a spiritual practice common in both ancient Greek and Indian cultures. The Greeks called this *omphaloskepsis*, a contemplation of the navel that was used as an aid to meditation and communion with divinity. Yogis also undertake this practice and activate the Manipura, or solar plexus chakra (see pages 44–45), to gain insight into the nature of the Universe. This chakra center has, in the Western alternative spiritual tradition, been associated with power and purpose. It is considered the seat of will.

You should protect this power center through practical techniques such as rubbing salt over your belly button when having energy-cleansing baths, or wearing a peace silk belt around your waist, under your clothes. Most important of all, keep your gut in good health by following a nutritious diet and paying attention to the foods and drinks that disagree with your digestive system.

CHAPTER 3

Yoga practice

Often there is an assumption that you need to attend classes, buy expensive yoga clothes, mats, blocks and all manner of other equipment in order to practice *asanas*. The truth is that, while yoga classes are useful for ensuring you are doing the postures correctly, you can learn yoga easily. Many people have a daily practice based on watching videos online, while others practice from books. All you really need is comfortable clothing that you can move freely in, and a non-slip, comfortable surface to practice on—this doesn't need to be a yoga mat; you could just use an ordinary rug if it is non-slip. Yoga is always practiced in bare feet.

A morning yoga practice feels very different from an evening one. Begin with 10 minutes each morning and build your practice from that.

Don't practice on a full stomach, and make sure you are sufficiently hydrated. It is good to begin alternate-nostril breathing, as this balances your body and builds a beginning to your *asanas* or postures. On the following pages, there are some simple postures that can help the cleansing of your chakras or the healing of your aura. You can use them as recommended elsewhere for specific problems, or as the core of a regular yoga practice.

CHAPTER 3

ALTERNATE-NOSTRIL BREATHING

1. Sit cross-legged on the floor, with your back upright. You can use a pillow or cushion to support you if you need it. If you find it hard to sit on the floor, you can sit on a chair. Just be sure to place your feet flat on the ground, hip-width apart.

2. Close your eyes if you feel comfortable doing so. If not, you can leave them shuttered slightly, maintaining a soft gaze.

3. Put your left hand gently on your lap, palm up.

4. Exhale completely and bring the thumb of your right hand up to your right nostril to close it.

5. Inhale through your left nostril and then block it with your little and ring fingers; release your right nostril and exhale out of it.

BALANCING YOUR AURA

6 You can rest your index and middle fingers on the third eye.

7 Inhale through the right nostril and close it again with your thumb. Release your left nostril and exhale out of it. This is now one full cycle of alternate-nostril breathing.

8 You can do this for about five minutes or for a number of cycles, but always finish a complete cycle.

This breathing exercise, called *nadi shodhana pranayama,* is a powerful way to balance your energies and focus your mind. It helps with anxiety, lowers stress, and helps your respiratory and cardiovascular systems. It promotes overall wellbeing and is a good daily practice to maintain. However, you should not practice this if you have a cold. And if you have asthma, a lung issue, or any other ailment that affects your breathing, speak to your doctor before you do this exercise.

CHAPTER 3

Prevention, not cure

Yoga is based on the principle that you should prevent illness through a regular practice rather than cure yourself when you are sick. Alla Svirinskaya is a fifth-generation energy healer from Russia who champions sustainable wellness. She says, "It is about wellness as a necessity. Like taking a shower or brushing your teeth. This is a necessity. It is also your necessity to be well. It's not a luxurious aspiration.

"Often, people discover spirituality or go to their doctors or healers when they're at breaking point. Only then, they do something. They're clearing their energy and doing energy rebalancing when they're completely overwhelmed and feel very toxic within. I don't want energy work and energy clearing to be as a desperate SOS kind of measure. What I'm trying to achieve is that people start looking at prophylactics for prevention as part of their daily routine."

Alla makes an excellent point. Ideally, we should not be clearing and balancing our auras once we are already sick; good energetic health should be a daily concern. The following yoga *asanas* will help you prevent energetic illnesses when practiced regularly.

CHAPTER 3

MOUNTAIN POSE

1. Stand with your feet hip-width apart. Ensure your feet are parallel.

2. Root down with the heels and the balls of your feet, spread and extend your toes, and draw up the arches of your feet.

3. Draw your knees and thigh muscles upwards.

4. Press the tops of the inner thighs back and the tailbone forward. Draw the lower abdomen and navel in and up.

5. Lengthen the spine upwards, lift the breastbone, allowing the shoulders to relax back and down; broaden the chest.

6. Lift the crown of the head while pressing the soles of the feet down, particularly the heels and the mounds of the toes, into the ground.

7. Extend your arms down the sides of the body, palms facing your thighs. Gaze straight ahead and breathe steadily. Remain in the pose for 20 seconds.

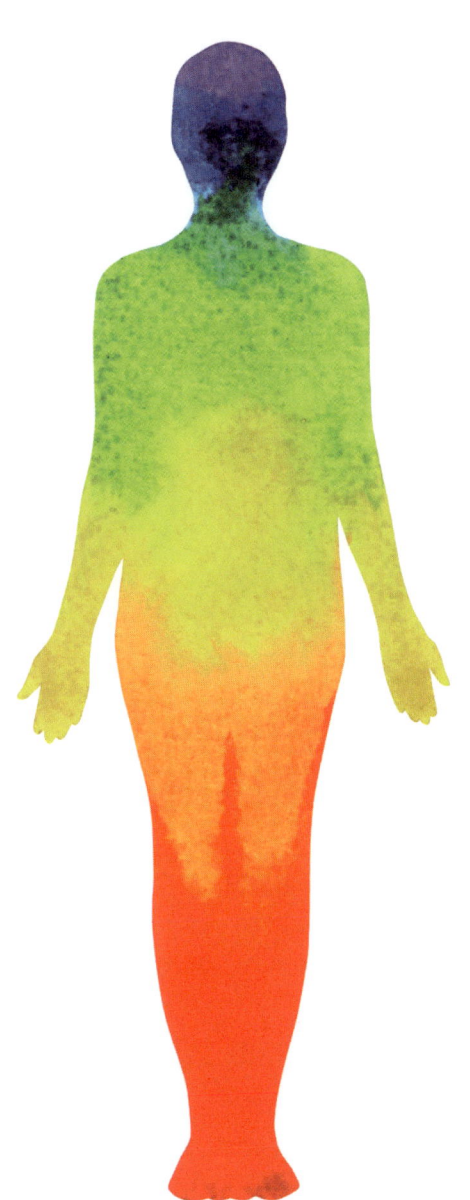

CHAPTER 3

TREE POSE

1 Stand in mountain pose (see page 76).

2 Put your weight on your left foot; raise your right leg and bend it at the knee. Place your raised foot on the inner thigh or the inner shin of your left leg. (Avoid placing the foot on the inner knee.) Your toes should be pointing downwards.

3 Join your palms together above your head. If this feels too difficult, you can bring your hands down into prayer position in front of you.

4 If you feel unstable, place a hand on the wall for support.

5 Let your spine lengthen upwards as you press the foot of your standing leg firmly down.

6 Feel the sense of being grounded as you root down.

7 Gaze straight ahead at eye level. This will help you balance.

8 Stay as long as feels comfortable; return to mountain pose.

9 Repeat on the other side.

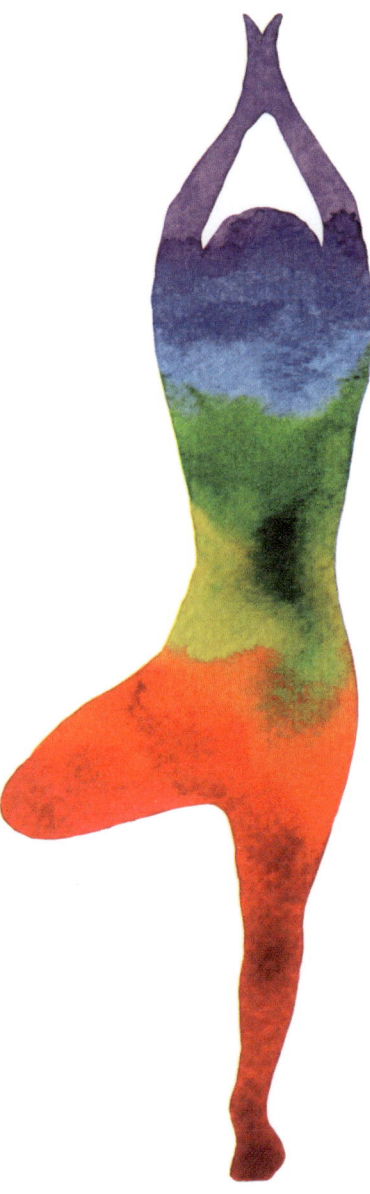

CHAPTER 3

WARRIOR POSE

1   Stand in mountain pose (see page 76).

2   Turn to the side of your mat and extend your feet approximately 3-4 feet apart.

3   Raise your arms above your head, palms facing each other. Yours arms should be straight and shoulder-width apart. (If your shoulders are tight or uncomfortable, take your arms wider apart.)

4   Turn your right foot 90 degrees to the right, and turn your back foot in to the right.

5   Bend your right knee. Your right knee should be positioned over your right heel, not collapsing inwards and not going beyond the heel.

6   Press down on your left outer heel; press your inner left thigh back; take your tailbone forwards. Stretch your body upwards. Gaze straight ahead.

7   Hold for 15-20 seconds, then come up out of the pose. Repeat on the other side.

CHAPTER 3

COBRA POSE

1. Lie prone (front-side down) on the floor.

2. Stretch your legs back and press the front of your thighs and feet into the ground. Draw your tailbone to the ground.

3. Place your hands flat on the floor by the sides of your chest with your elbows hugging the sides of your body.

BALANCING YOUR AURA

4 On an inhalation, start to lift your chest off the ground by pressing your hands firmly down and starting to straighten the arms.

5 Draw the navel up toward the chest, drop the shoulders down away from the ears, lift the sternum without the front ribs flaring.

6 Ensure the backbend is evenly distributed throughout the spine to avoid putting pressure on the lower back.

7 Do not strain the back by trying to come up too high. Keeping the elbows bent rather than straightening the arms completely will help avoid potential strain.

8 Stay in the pose for up to 30 seconds; then, on an exhalation, lower your body down and rest.

CHAPTER 3

CHILD'S POSE

1. Kneel down on all fours.

2. Your knees should be slightly more than hip-width apart. Bring your big toes together. Move your sitting bones back to rest on your heels. You can place a rolled-up blanket or towel under your feet if there is discomfort in the front of the feet, and/or, similarly, between the backs of your thighs and your calves if your sitting bones don't reach your heels.

3   On an exhalation, bend forward from the hips, keeping the front of your body long, and rest your torso between your thighs.

4   Place your forehead on the ground, or, if it does not reach the ground, rest your forehead on a block (or book). Your head should not hang without support. Observe the place where your forehead meets the ground or support.

5   Extend your arms out in front of you, palms face-down.

6   This is a resting pose — there should be no discomfort in your knees, legs, shoulders or back. Let your breath be easy and fluid.

7   Rest in this position for up to 2 minutes.

8   Exit the pose on an inhalation, pressing your hands into the floor to lift up your body.

CHAPTER 3

CORPSE POSE

This is the ultimate pose for balancing all your energy centers and bringing yourself back into alignment. It is a good *asana* to finish your practice on.

1. Sit on the floor and extend your legs out in front of you. Then slowly lower yourself to the ground until you are lying supine on the floor.

2. Let your arms and legs fall away from the sides of your body. Turn your palms to face the ceiling, and let your legs and feet relax out to the sides. Ensure your limbs are as symmetrical as possible to enable optimal relaxation.

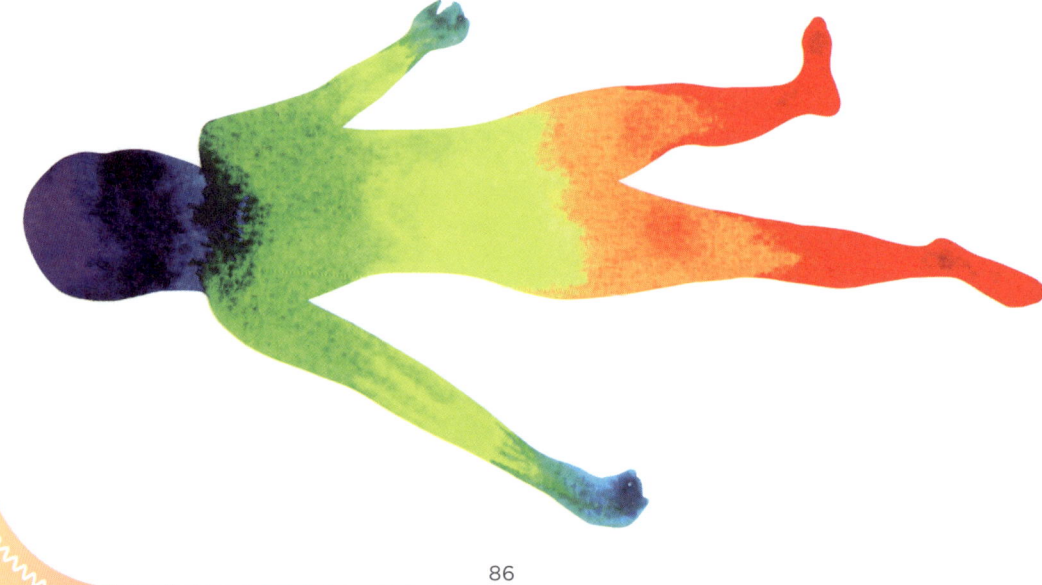

BALANCING YOUR AURA

3 Place a pillow under your knees if there is any tension in your back; alternatively, you can support the lower legs on the seat of a chair.

4 Place a folded blanket under your head and neck if your head is tilted backwards.

5 Close your eyes and allow your body to relax; surrender the weight of the body to the ground beneath you.

6 Keep your attention on your breathing, and try to remain completely still.

7 Stay in the pose for up to 5 minutes, then slowly bring your awareness back, open your eyes, draw your knees up and over to the right and then push yourself up to a seated position.

Hand healing

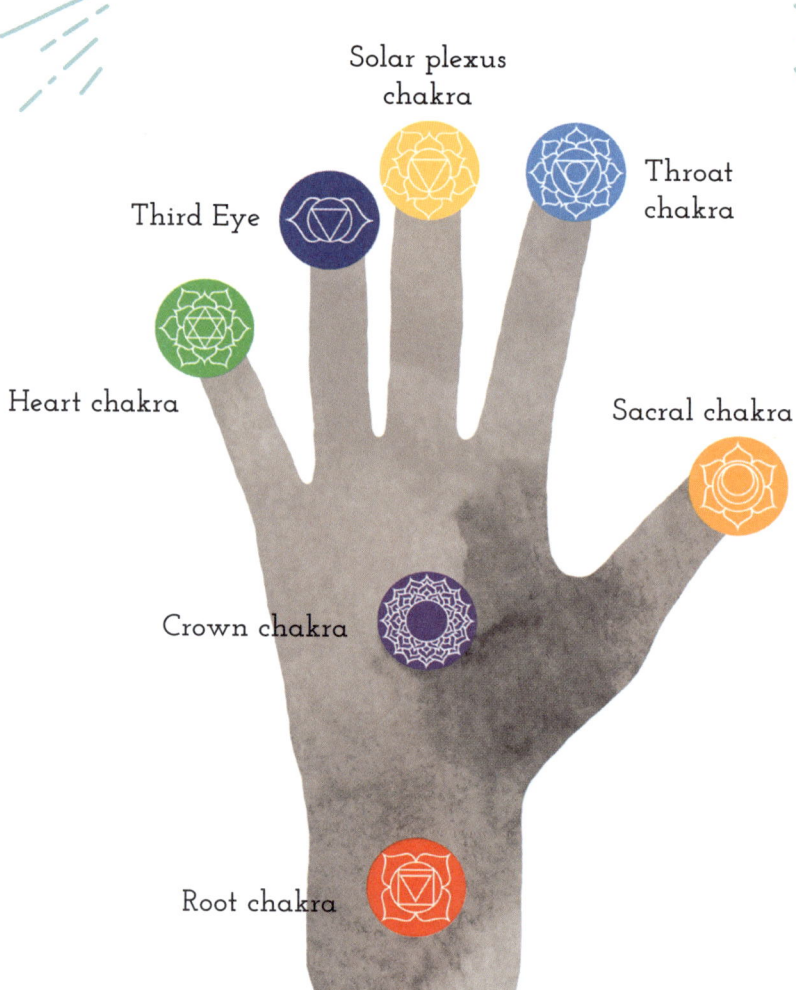

BALANCING YOUR AURA

One of the best ways you can balance your aura is through your hands. The aura is denser here, so your hands should be more naturally protected than other parts of your body. Hands are also connected to all the organs and energy points in your body, so manipulating your hands can help you heal that part of your body and your life.

However, you can also impart healing through hands-on touch. We have already seen the beneficial effects of massage, but once you are able to view the aura, you will also be able to direct energy through your hands to balance and heal the other person's aura.

You can visualize opening your hands' chakras by shaking them gently in front of you with the palms facing toward you. You can also do so by rubbing your hands vigorously together until they feel warm and tingly. That sensation is an indication that you have activated the chakras of your hands and can apply them to draw energy from the universal source into whoever you are healing.

HENNA CIRCLES

A simple henna design, such as the one shown, is often used in the subcontinent to cool the hands (and consequently the hand chakras) as well as to attract prosperity and good luck to the wearer. Henna is a natural dye that has been used around the world in rites and rituals.

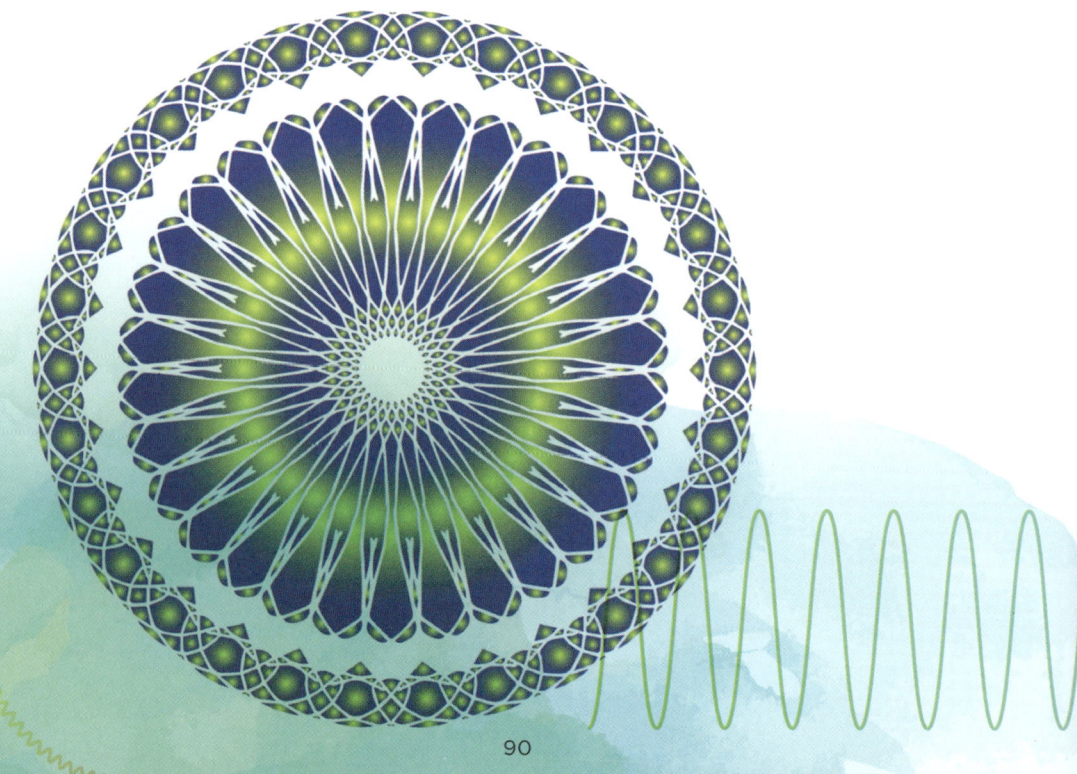

CHAPTER 3

ENERGY SPHERE

One of the ways you can both sense and balance your aura is to do the following exercise.

1. Sit in a straight-backed chair with your feet flat on the floor.

2. Hold your hands out in front of you with the palms facing inwards.

3. Draw your hands in until they are an inch apart, but not touching.

4. Feel the sensation of resistance between your palms. This is your aura's energy that you're feeling.

5. Move your hands apart and together again until you get a clearer sensation of the energy between them.

6. You can then visualize that energy forming a sphere that you are holding in your hands like a ball.

7   Within that ball of light, visualize your entire body with a strong, healthy aura around it.

8   Finally, send that energetic sphere up to the heavens above your head.

CHAPTER 4

CHAPTER 4

Your sacred space

Have you ever been in the midst of a city crowd? Most of us feel very uncomfortable in such a situation. This is because there are several auras chaotically assaulting the borders of our own aura. On occasion, if your own aura is weak, you will attract people and situations that cause irritation and frustration in daily life. A delayed train. An impatient commuter shoving you out of the way. Spilt coffee.

The way to prevent this from happening is to ensure that you are recharging somewhere that is completely in alignment with your energy body. Your home may not currently be a sacred space in the way that a church or temple might be, but you should aim to get it there. You can create a sacred space more or less anywhere, but there are certain things you should do when you're first starting to clear your space.

DECLUTTER AND DETOX

While it's fine to have a lot of possessions or collections, clutter is not good for your aura or the auras of the people and animals that live in your home. Clutter can be defined as something you don't need and don't love. People often harm their auras by not handling their clutter. This is because clutter essentially represents decisions that haven't been made. So every time you see that stack of papers that hasn't been filed, or that pile of clothes that hasn't been donated or washed, you feel guilt. Guilt is toxic to your aura. Prolonged guilt will damage your aura, so you must address it as soon as possible.

Having cleared your clutter (and get help if you find it too stressful to deal with by yourself), you should give everything in your home a spring clean. Do not use harsh chemicals, as they inevitably hurt both your physical body and your auric one. There are many natural ingredients, including baking soda, lemon and vinegar, that are good for cleaning; also, there are plenty of health-food stores that stock natural, chemical-free household cleaners.

THE ENVIRONMENT AND OTHER PEOPLE

Once this is done, you'll find that the energy has shifted somewhat in your home. At this point, you can dedicate it to your highest good by smudging (see pages 25–26) and stating your intention to create a nourishing, safe and happy home.

Then, walk from your front door clockwise around each room in your house, holding your hands out in front of you. Try to sense the energy of your furniture, possessions, décor and layout. Does anything feel a bit "sticky," or as if it's in the wrong place? Now is a good time to rearrange furniture or thin out artwork if it doesn't feel right.

COLORS AND THEMES

Blues are among the most calming and aura-friendly colors to have in your home. White is also very soothing. However, do not reject reds and oranges automatically, as a deep red bedroom can be reminiscent of the womb and can therefore feel very safe and cozy. Orange is also great for kitchens, as it stimulates the appetite and aids digestion.

Choose patterns, motifs and themes with care, as each has meaning and consequences for how you will feel in your space. Generally, materials such as wood and textiles are better for the human aura than metal and plastic, so try to make sure that pieces of furniture, such as your bed, are made of wood.

Share your space with plants and animals, if you can. Ferns and spider plants are great air purifiers, and have calming auras that will ensure the overall atmosphere in your house remains clean and uplifting.

CHAPTER 4

Pets are excellent at reading auras, and will naturally gravitate toward those whose auras indicate that they are friendly and good. They also sense when you need a cuddle due to emotional distress, and will attempt to cheer you up without prompting.

DIGITAL DETOX

It is not practical to recommend that you do away with all digital devices, since most of our lives are now lived on apps and mobile phones. However, you should put away your phone when doing two vital things: sleeping and eating. The electromagnetism that mobile phones emit when in use affect our auras badly. It is simple enough to leave your phone charging in a different room when you go to bed. You should also put down the phone and turn off the TV when you're eating. You can help this process by having a dining table or a dedicated place where you sit to eat. Make meals sacrosanct, and always give your full attention to the process of nourishing your body.

When items like TVs, computers and stereos are not in use, turn them off at the socket rather than leaving them on sleep. This is to ensure that any electromagnetic frequencies are kept to a minimum in your home. If you want to get really radical in the pursuit of a clear aura, consider not having a TV at all. I know a number of very happy people who don't have one.

CHAPTER 4

Places of power

There are some people who return again and again to the same vacation destination each year. They visit the same bars and restaurants, see the same sights, and enjoy the same activities at around the same time each year. You may consider them unadventurous, but actually they are very fortunate for, generally speaking, these are people who have found the aura of a place that agrees with their own personal energy makeup.

If you manage to find a place that attracts you and makes you feel great, it may well be your own personal place of power. You feel invigorated there; your shoulders relax, as does your jaw, and you feel as though you have been transported to a delightful place.

FINDING YOUR PLACE IN THE WORLD

There are some obvious contenders for finding a place to give you solace. Stone circles have traditionally been centers of energy and ritual for Pagan and Neolithic communities in Britain and Ireland. These are powerful, not just because of where they're located (usually built along energetic lines that are particularly potent), but also because the aura of a place is influenced by its history. Where sacred rituals and rites have taken place, the area takes on an aura of power and transcendence that is almost magical. This is, on occasion, ruined by human beings when they commodify the experience and turn it into a gimmick or a novelty, but you can still find amazing places off the beaten track that align to the cravings of our auras.

Stone circles have fascinating auras that join to create a shield around the whole area.

CHAPTER 4

Water is another attraction for the human aura. Oceanfront and riverside properties always cost more money because of the truism that we are attracted to water. Moving water will keep the energy of a place clear and light, while stagnant water in ponds or manmade lakes can exude melancholy due to the lack of connection with the world's water system.

However, not all manmade structures suffer from this problem. Wells and portals or holes made in stone act as energy points from which you

The Sufi monastery of Blagaj Tekke in Blagaj, Bosnia, is built next to the source of the river Buna. Rivers and moving water are classic ways to tap into the energy of the Earth.

Wells and stone portals act like the chakras of the Earth, allowing energy to pool and move outward into the world.

can draw energy into the world. In myth and legend, we often hear of these holes, and know to fear and respect their power. Passing through a stone circle almost always leads you to the fairy world, so these gateways have a touch of the magical to them.

If you find a place of power that resonates with you, but you are unable to visit it as often as you like, you can connect with it using the meditation on pages 146–149. This is a great way to enhance your auric connection to the area, and you may find that opportunities begin to

CHAPTER 4

open up that will lead you to being able to visit it in real life soon.

If you find that you are living in a part of the world that doesn't agree with you or your aura, you will never be able to find happiness until you leave, so you must work to bring about that change. This can't be done by criticizing or denigrating the place where you live. It can only be done by praising the place where you think you will be happier. Attraction rather than rejection must be your operating procedure.

THE ENVIRONMENT AND OTHER PEOPLE

Helping others

Healing your friends and family is an act that not only helps them, but also helps you. This is because if you could see your aura, you would see tendrils of energy stretching out and connecting you with everyone you know. Some tendrils, for example those connecting you to your life partner, are like thick cords that connect you strongly to another person's energy. Others, like those connecting you to the cashier at your local supermarket, are faint but nevertheless present. Whenever we think about someone, a tendril zooms out and connects with their energy. It doesn't matter how physically far away that person is—the tendril will still find them. Some religions believe that when you pray for your dead, the prayer energy reaches the person in heaven and gives them both pleasure and merit.

TEA AND SYMPATHY

While not every person you love will want to explore the world of auras with you, you can help heal their aura by doing something quite mundane. Sharing tea with someone is an easy way to connect with their energy, give them some of your healing vibes, and make them feel loved.

These teas are particularly good for the aura:
- Chamomile
- Rosehip
- Nettle
- Peppermint
- Jasmine

AFFIRMATIONS

If you have a friend who is a little more open-minded about auric healing, you can try partnered affirmations. An affirmation is a positive, present-timed statement of what you would like to manifest in your life. When you say them aloud with a friend who repeats them back to you, it creates an auric bond that makes the outcome far more likely. This is because there is

THE ENVIRONMENT AND OTHER PEOPLE

someone else witnessing your affirmation and confirming it back to you.

So you might say, "I am strong and healthy." Then your friend says to you, "You are strong and healthy."

Or you might do an affirmation to manifest wealth or a loving relationship. What you choose to affirm is up to you, but the statement must be in the present tense, so no "I will be…". And it must be positive, so no

CHAPTER 4

statements that begin "I am not…"

After you say your affirmations to each other and repeat them back to each other, make a note of what you said and the date when you said it; then look back once your outcomes have manifested. Did anything not manifest? What do you or your friend believe is blocking that outcome for you both? How can you convince yourself?

For example, suppose you affirmed "I am fit enough to run a marathon," but you didn't manage to run one despite your friend affirming it back to you. It may be that you are fit enough to run a marathon, but you didn't affirm that you have successfully completed a marathon. Or it may be that you have done nothing beyond the affirmation to meet your goal. The affirmation will help, but you still need to put in the training sessions. Reaffirm your goal and report back to your friend each time you undertake a training session so that your friend is also convinced that your goal will be met.

Interestingly, Alla Svirinskaya, the hugely talented Russian medical doctor and healer mentioned earlier, has discovered that it is best to say affirmations in the language you used from when you learned to talk until around the age of 10. For me this is Punjabi and, in learning this nugget of useful information, I found my affirmations moved up a level as a result of saying them in Punjabi.

ABSENCE OF AN AURA

In your early days of trying to see auras, you may find that you do not see anything at all—and that is absolutely fine. However, some say that the absence of an aura can be a sign of impending death. The famous psychic Edgar Cayce wrote of a very sad and dramatic experience in his pamphlet *Auras*. He had been shopping in a department store and was going to take the elevator. As the doors opened, he felt a dark hollowness inside it, despite it being quite full of people. At that exact moment, a red sweater caught his eye, and he motioned for the elevator to leave without him, intending to catch the next one. The cable snapped on the elevator and all the occupants plunged to their deaths. Cayce wrote how odd the whole experience had been, since he didn't even like the color red. Thankfully, in our explorations of auras, not seeing an aura will not mean anything other than that we need a lot more practice.

CHAPTER 5

CHAPTER 5

Vital energy

You should appreciate that your aura is ever-changing and your energy body is forever moving and leaping with your changing emotions, thoughts and behaviors. However, your aura needs regular replenishment with vital energy. A healthy person replenishes their energy through exercise, being in nature, and engaging in activities that elevate their consciousness. An unhealthy person drains their energy and causes damage to their aura through overwork, bad diet, and engaging in criticism of both themselves and others.

I have never watched drama-infused TV shows because I feel that they harm the psyche. The louder and more aggressive a program is, the more you will attract that sort of behavior into your life, because your aura begins to reorder itself into the shape of the damaged aura of someone who has a lot of drama and conflict in their life.

You can draw lots of healing energy from nature due to its superabundant ability to replenish auras.

CHAPTER 5

Energy Vampirism

It is not just a diet of bad TV and overwork that damages your aura. On occasion, illness, trauma or certain psychic practices can cause "wounds" in the aura where energy leaks out and depletes a person's vital life force. This can cause them to, quite unconsciously, seek energy sources that are not appropriate. Chiefly, this means draining others of their vital energy. When you are with such people, you may find that you feel exhausted and low afterwards, while they go away feeling refreshed and replenished. This is because the energy drain has left you depleted while they have been topped up with your vital force.

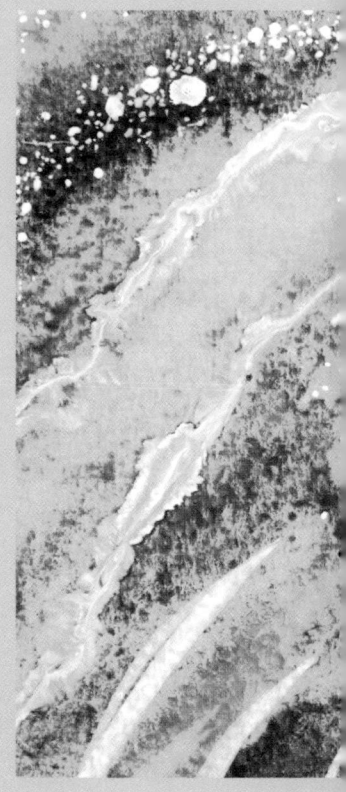

What can you do about this? Don't, whatever you do, accuse your friend or acquaintance of being an energy vampire! Nobody will respond well to such an accusation, and the vast majority of people have no idea that they're doing this. Your best bet is to keep your time with them to a minimum and make your way to a place of natural beauty soon after you have seen them, as trees are natural super-producers of vital energy, and taking some of that vital force from them will harm neither the trees nor yourself.

ENERGETIC PROTECTION

You can even be drained of energy on the phone or a video call. The person does not need to be in the room with you to drain your energy. This is a characteristic of the fact that energy does not follow the rules of physical engagement, but is on a different, more mobile plane.

ENERGETIC PROTECTION

Cord-cutting

If you find that you continue to feel depleted by a particular person and, after seeing them, no amount of time with trees is helping, you can choose to do a cord-cutting. As we saw earlier, every time we think of someone, a tendril of light energy connects us to them. Often if we begin to dread seeing someone, those tendrils become stronger, as we are still thinking about them—even if negatively.

If you are ready to have that person leave your life entirely—for example, in the case of an abusive ex—then you can do a cord-cutting. This is where you cut the energetic ties connecting you to a person and it results in a real-life break from them. Sit in meditation in the way that the meditations chapter teaches (pages 124–155) and think about the person. Then imagine the new tendril connecting you to that person. This will enable you to view the cord that is tying you to them. Imagine a white light sword in your mind's eye, and have it swiftly and cleanly cut through the cord. Imagine that your end of the cord retreats back into your whole and healed aura. You do not have to visualize it, but you can rest assured that their end of the cord has also retreated to their own energy body.

Once this is done, make a conscious effort to avoid thinking about, communicating or talking about the person. You have now moved on energetically and physically.

CHAPTER 5

Thought-forms

The pineal gland is what enables thoughts to reach out into the world and manifest. It is used extensively in clairvoyance. Our auras can retain both positive and negative thought-forms within them, sometimes manifesting to those with psychic sight as symbols in the aura. Negative thought-forms can cause many problems in the physical world, as they are the result of painful or unhelpful beliefs. If you were told that you were stupid as a child, that thought-form can get trapped in your aura and needs to be released if you are to regain your psychic protection. You can release this form through an affirmation, an auric healing with a practitioner, or through a period of meditation.

You can then replace negative thought-forms with strong, positive ones. If you can create an impression in your mind of an outcome that is desirable to you, and put enough passion behind it, it will arise as a thought-form that must manifest in real life.

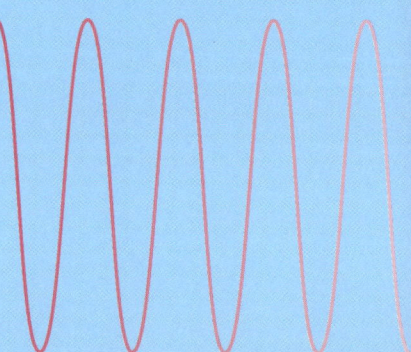

CHAPTER 5

Attracting the wrong people

Before she met her husband, my eldest daughter attracted the strangest, most arrogant, difficult men in the northern hemisphere. One evening she brought home another terrible date who was rude and dismissive. So, naturally, I scolded her. Now, before you worry that I am an awful father, my children have been brought up to understand energy. They know that if they are attracting things that are wrong for them, there is definitely something happening there energetically that is not just bad luck.

"Why do you think that this is the sort of person you deserve in a relationship?" I asked her.

When we drilled down into the truth of it, it appeared that she had an erroneous belief that she wasn't attractive enough to get the best men to date her. When I asked her how and when she had started believing this thoroughly incorrect thought, she realized that it was a lie she had been telling herself since her teenage years. She released it, and her wonderful husband came into her life very quickly and very easily. In much the same way, when you release the wrong, negative thought-forms from your aura, you will attract what is best for you.

ENERGETIC PROTECTION

Intuitive scanning

You should get into the habit of intuitively scanning situations before you enter them. If you get to the stage where you can see auras quite clearly, you will find that you can just soften your eyes and see the information you need from a scenario—for example, whether to get the oncoming train or the one after it.

You may find that you can't visually see anything and, in such a case, you should develop your intuition to give you the same helpful information. If you are faced with two paths, you can, at the point of choice, "feel" which is the best one for you. Ensuring you are regularly engaging in the cleansing practices on pages 25–31 will help you develop that intuitive sense.

CHAPTER 6

The meditations

CHAPTER 6

Meditation to see your own aura

Do not be discouraged if, the first time you do this meditation, you are unable to see your aura. It is said that it takes at least 42 days of daily meditation before you can fully see changes in energy—so a regular practice is vitally important.

THE MEDITATIONS

1. Ensure that you are in a calm mood. Sip water. Breathe in and out in a gentle, conscious, yet unforced way.

2. Once you have reached a feeling of calm, close your eyes and state your intention to see your energy body.

3. Keeping your eyes closed, place your hands, one over the other, at your belly button with the palm of the hand closest to your body resting gently on your stomach.

4. As you breathe in and out, imagine that there is a force field of light that is emanating from your body on the in breath and contracting toward your body on the out breath. This may seem counterintuitive, but energy follows the physical body and, as you breathe out, your lungs deflate and your chest cavity gets smaller, thereby bringing your energy body closer to your physical body.

5. In your imagination, start at the top of your head and "scan" down your body, looking for any areas where the energy feels different. Is there stagnation around your shoulder blades? Does your energy feel fragmented around an old injury? Keep going until you reach the soles of your feet.

6. Now open your eyes, and hold your hands out in front of you with the palms facing toward you. If you are wearing a ring,

leave it on, and look at the dividing space between the ring and your finger. Soften your eyes and see if you can see a blurring at the edges of your hands. Do you get any impression of color or shapes, lines or textures here?

7 After a few minutes, rub your palms together, close your eyes and place your hands over your eyes to soothe them.

8 Record your impressions of what you saw or thought about during the meditation in a journal. Do this for at least a month, and look back to see if any insights about your energy have emerged.

TIPS

❖ Ensure you practice your meditation at the same time each day.

❖ Try and sit on an upright chair with your feet flat on the ground and your back supported by the back of the chair.

❖ Ideally, sit in front of a white or light-colored wall. If this is not possible, ensure there is no visual clutter in front of you.

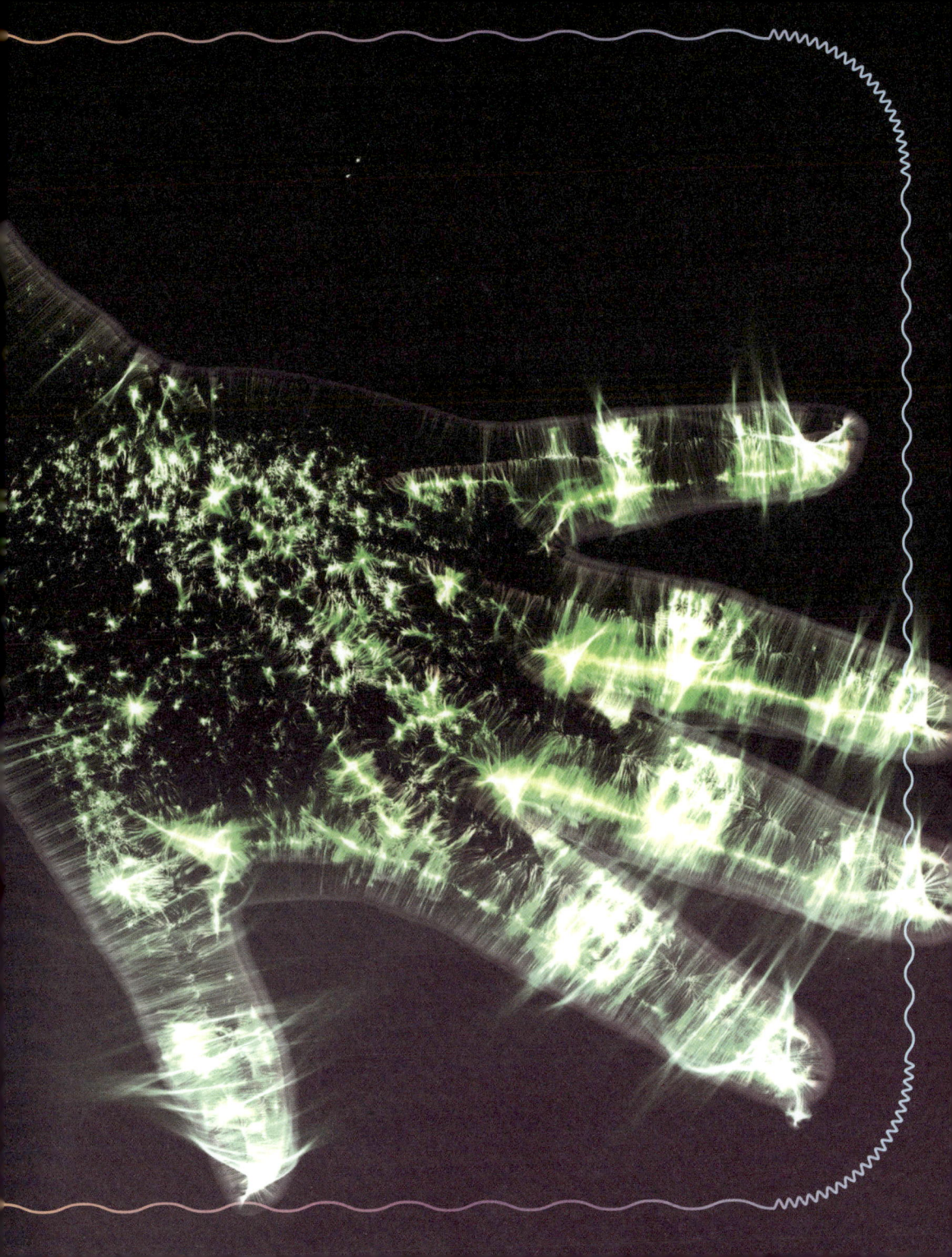

CHAPTER 6

Meditation to see the auras of others

Seeing the auras of others will help you understand them better and feel more compassion for them. However, it is best to practice this meditation alone and then try to see a friend's aura first before trying with strangers. The sort of "seeing" this requires will make it look like you are staring at or beyond people and, in some cultures, this can be considered rude—so be aware of how you practice this skill.

1. Ensure that you are in a calm mood. Sip water. Breathe in and out in a gentle, conscious, yet unforced way.

2. Once you have reached a feeling of calm, close your eyes and state your intention to be able to see the auras of others.

3. Keeping your eyes closed, place your hands, one over the other, at your belly button with the palm of the hand closest to your body resting gently on your stomach.

4. As you breathe in and out, imagine that there is a force field of light that is emanating from your body on the in breath and

contracting toward your body on the out breath. Then rest your hands, palms up, on your lap.

5 In your imagination, see a tower of light entering into the top of your head. This is a white sparkling column of light and, as you gaze with your mind's eye, you can see that the column goes up into a web or net high above you. That web has many, many columns of light connecting to other people all over the world. You cannot see above the web of light, but you can see that it connects all people together.

6 Look down the column of light to the person nearest to you (you may find that you get the impression of it being a friend or close relation, or someone you live with). Imagine there is a sheath of light around their body. What does it look like? Is it clear? Any colors, gaps or breaks in their energy body? Where are those gaps?

7 Thank them for allowing you to observe their energy, and give them a blessing for their highest good (even if this is a person you do not get along with in daily life).

8 Turn your palms downward on your lap and rub them against your thighs. Gently open your eyes when you are ready.

AFTER THE MEDITATION

Ask a friend if you can try and look at their aura. It may even be the person you saw in your meditation, but it doesn't have to be. Seat them in front of a light-colored wall, or at least a clutter-free background. Soften your eyes and "scan" their body from top to bottom. Look for colors, movement in the energy, gaps or filaments of light. Do not attempt to interpret what any of this means, and don't panic your friend by saying you can see gaps in their energy! Ask questions about any parts you see unusual energy around, just to see if you're picking up on anything they may have experienced. For example, if you see a grayish color around their knees, ask them how their knees are. You may find they have arthritis or knee pain. Over time, you will be able to check over anyone's aura just by adjusting how you look at them.

THE MEDITATIONS

Meditation to connect with your houseplants

Sometimes we have a houseplant that, no matter what we do, seems determined to die. It may be that it is energetically not for us, and we may be better off giving it to someone who it might thrive with. However, if you want to connect with your plants in a more meaningful way, you can also try this meditation. You do not need to have the ailing plant in front of you, but it may help your visualization if it is in the same room.

1   Ensure that you are in a calm mood. Sip water. Breathe in and out in a gentle, conscious, yet unforced way.

2   Once you have reached a feeling of calm, close your eyes and state your intention to energetically connect with your plants.

3   Keeping your eyes closed, place your hands, one over the other, at your belly button with the palm of the hand closest to your body resting gently on your stomach.

4 As you breathe in and out, imagine that there is a force field of light that is emanating from your body on the in breath and contracting toward your body on the out breath. Then rest your hands, palms up, on your lap.

5 In your mind's eye, visualize a leaf. It can be the shape of a leaf of the plant you wish to connect with or it can be a generic leaf to represent all plants. The only important thing is that you see it clearly in your mind's eye.

6 See a light emanating from the leaf, causing it to glow from within. Note any colors or filaments and any impressions that occur about the energy of plants.

7 Thank the "spirit of plants," for that is what you've been connecting with, for allowing you to observe its energy and give a blessing to all plants, especially those living in your home. You can also concentrate on sending healing thoughts to any plant in your home that is particularly unwell.

8 Turn your palms downward on your lap and rub them against your thighs. Gently open your eyes when you are ready.

THE MEDITATIONS

Meditation to see through the eyes of an animal

Many animals see things radically differently from humans. For example, bees can see ultraviolet light that humans can't see. Scent can almost be "seen" by dogs and cats since it is so pronounced and is a marker for territory. Birds can see the Earth's magnetic field. It can be good to sometimes "see" through the eyes of an animal, as it gives you another perspective into the invisible energies that are all around us.

1 Ensure that you are in a calm mood. Sip water. Breathe in and out in a gentle, conscious, yet unforced way.

2 Once you have reached a feeling of calm, close your eyes and state your intention to be able to see through the eyes of an animal.

3 Keeping your eyes closed, place your hands, one over the other, at your belly button with the palm of the hand closest to your body resting gently on your stomach.

4 As you breathe in and out, imagine that there is a force field of light that is emanating from your body on the in breath and contracting toward your body on the out breath. Then rest your hands, palms up, on your lap.

5 Think of the animal whose eyes you'd like to see through. It is better if you pick a wild animal that is representative of all of its species and is not in your life. It is a bad idea to pick a pet, as your pets already have an energetic link to you and may not like the sensation of you connecting with them in that way.

6 Visualize how that animal sounds, looks, moves and eats. Imagine it doing a normal everyday action such as eating, and then imagine that you're seeing the food it's eating because you are looking out from its eyes. Is it a predator or prey animal? Do you see what is in front of you or to the sides? Can you see colors? Lines of energy?

7 Once you have noted your impressions, thank the animal for permitting you to look out of its eyes for a while, and send blessings to all animals.

8 Turn your palms downward on your lap and rub them against your thighs. Gently open your eyes when you are ready.

THE MEDITATIONS

Meditation to attract loving relationships

This meditation works irrespective of whether you're single, attached, or not interested in romantic relationships at all. It is to attract a loving quality in *all* your relationships including parents, siblings, friends, colleagues and acquaintances. It is likely to find you fostering a friendlier connection even with strangers you meet, including commuters on your train or the person who sells you your monthly travel pass.

1. Ensure that you are in a calm mood. Sip water. Breathe in and out in a gentle, conscious, yet unforced way.

2. Once you have reached a feeling of calm, close your eyes and state your intention to be able to attract and maintain loving relationships.

3. Keeping your eyes closed, place your hands, one over the other, at your belly button with the palm of the hand closest to your body resting gently on your stomach.

4. As you breathe in and out, imagine that there is a force field of

light that is emanating from your body on the in breath and contracting toward your body on the out breath. Then rest your hands, palms up, on your lap.

5 Imagine a column of rose-pink sparkling light coming down from the heavens and entering you at the top of your head.

6 Feel that light filling your body and emerging out of every pore. Feel the love that this light represents, and then imagine it emanating outward to encompass your family, your friends, your community, your country, your continent and your world.

7 Say out loud: "I walk in loving kindness; I speak with loving kindness; I act with loving kindness."

8 Turn your palms downward on your lap and rub them against your thighs. Gently open your eyes when you are ready.

CHAPTER 6

Meditation to attract wealth

Life can sometimes throw wildcards at you that affect your wealth and wellbeing. In such times, your aura reacts and you find yourself unable to be a good, clear vessel for holding money and prosperity. When this occurs, and you feel abundance slipping away, it is good to do this meditation to switch your aura back into attracting instead of repelling mode.

1   Ensure that you are in a calm mood. Sip water. Breathe in and out in a gentle, conscious, yet unforced way.

2   Once you have reached a feeling of calm, close your eyes and state your intention to be able to attract and maintain loving relationships.

3   Keeping your eyes closed, place your hands, one over the other, at your belly button with the palm of the hand closest to your body resting gently on your stomach.

4   As you breathe in and out, imagine that there is a force field of light that is emanating from your body on the in breath and

contracting towards your body on the out breath. Then rest your hands, palms up, on your lap.

5 Imagine a column of green jade-colored, sparkling light coming down from the heavens and entering you at the top of your head.

6 Feel that light filling your body and emerging out of every pore. Feel the prosperity and wealth that this light represents, and then imagine it emanating outward from you, where it magnetizes money and wealth opportunities, and draws them to you.

7 Say out loud: "I release lack; I am abundantly wealthy."

8 Turn your palms downward on your lap and rub them against your thighs. Gently open your eyes when you are ready.

THE MEDITATIONS

Meditation to heal your environment

We can sometimes feel powerless to affect our environment. We hear and see news that about the climate crisis, we can see plastic pollution in the oceans, and we worry about what the future will hold if our planet's ecosystem is unable to heal from the strain we have put on it. Doing this meditation can help you appreciate that we are all connected to each other and to the planet. Sending healing energy to the environment you live in is a pure endeavor that has benefits for all.

1. Ensure that you are in a calm mood. Sip water. Breathe in and out in a gentle, conscious, yet unforced way.

2. Once you have reached a feeling of calm, close your eyes and state your intention to be able to heal your environment.

3. Keeping your eyes closed, place your hands, one over the other, at your belly button with the palm of the hand closest to your body resting gently on your stomach.

CHAPTER 6

4   As you breathe in and out, imagine that there is a force field of light that is emanating from your body on the in breath and contracting toward your body on the out breath. Then rest your hands, palms up, on your lap.

5   Imagine a column of white light coming down from the heavens and entering you at the top of your head.

6   Feel that light filling your body and emerging out of every pore. As the light pours out of you, it begins to pool under your hands at your belly button. Move your hands to accommodate the pooling energy that begins to form a sphere in front of your stomach.

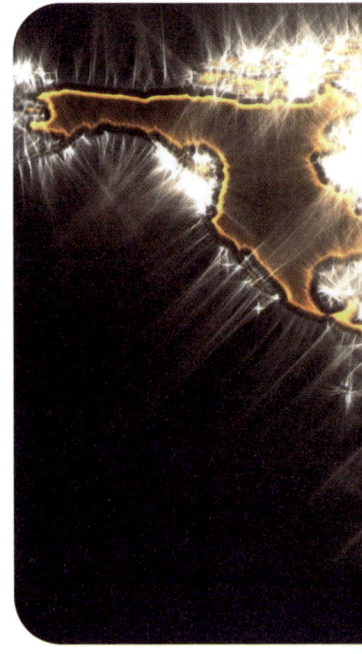

7   Within that ball of light, visualize the outcome that you would like for your environment. You could imagine walking along a pristine beach with no litter and no plastic in the ocean. Or you could imagine an abundant rainforest with the sound of birdsong and forest animals. Closer to home, you could visualize your community coming together to pick up litter or to create a public park or garden.

THE MEDITATIONS

8 Once you have you created that vision in your ball of light, physically guide the light up over your head and out into the divine dimensions.

9 Feel gratitude for living where you live and for having space in this dimension. Give thanks for all the energies in the spiritual realm who help you every day in your life.

10 Turn your palms downward on your lap and rub them against your thighs. Gently open your eyes when you are ready.

CHAPTER 6

Meditation to attract the right job/career

The hardest part of any job or career is making a decision about what it is that you want to do. Once you have that part figured out, you can formulate what you need to do to achieve that outcome, and your energy also aligns to attract it to you. However, if you don't know what it is that you want to do with your life, or you feel as though you've spent some time in the wrong career and aren't sure what it is you want to do—only what you *don't* want to do—then this meditation should help you get some clarity.

1. Ensure that you are in a calm mood. Sip water. Breathe in and out in a gentle, conscious, yet unforced way.

2. Once you have reached a feeling of calm, close your eyes and state your desire to attract a career that's right for you.

3. Keeping your eyes closed, place your hands, one over the other, at your belly button with the palm of the hand closest to your body resting gently on your stomach.

THE MEDITATIONS

4. As you breathe in and out, imagine that there is a force field of light that is emanating from your body on the in breath and contracting toward your body on the out breath. Then rest your hands, palms up, on your lap.

5. Imagine a column of sparkling yellow light coming down from the heavens and entering you at the top of your head.

6. Feel that light filling your body and emerging out of every pore. Let that light pool at your stomach and form a ball of light in your hands. Then, in your mind's eye, look into that ball of light as if you were looking into a crystal ball. See what comes up. Are you sitting at a desk, or are you outside? What are you wearing? Who are you working with? Try and see as much detail as possible.

7. Once you have seen some clear signs that may serve as leads for investigating a particular job or career, thank the Universe for the information, and push the ball of light above your head into the divine realm.

8. Then place your palms downward on your lap and rub them against your thighs. Gently open your eyes when you are ready.

CHAPTER 6

TIPS

Once you've been given some leads from this meditation about what you should be doing, remember to do some conscious research into what you've been shown.

◎ It may be that you saw an animal in your meditation. If so, this won't necessarily mean that you should become a vet or a zookeeper. It may be that you have to embody the qualities of the animal that you saw.

◎ Fill out some job applications and investigate employment agencies. While you might not know exactly what you want to do, your meditation will start to attract opportunities.

◎ Stay positive—don't give up!

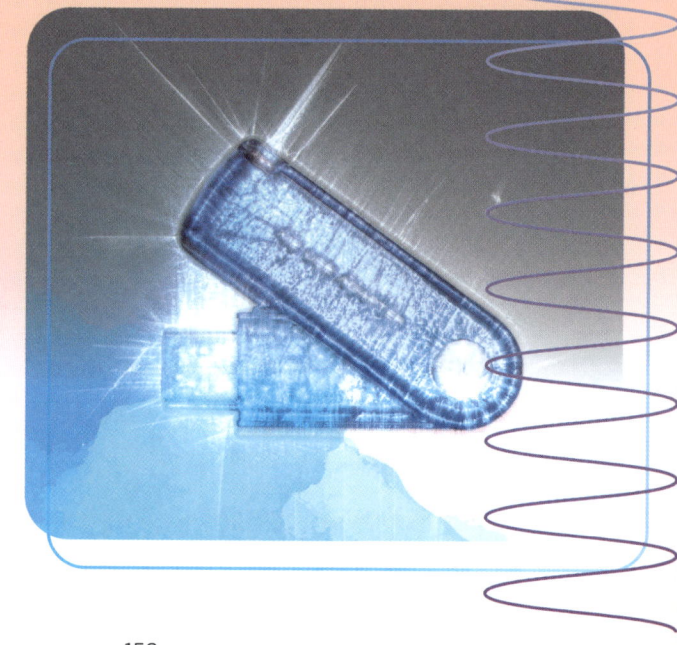

THE MEDITATIONS

Meditation to attract new opportunities

You may be trying to sell a property, or you may want to move to another country. However, you feel stagnated and can't see how to move forward with your plans. This meditation, when done every day for a month, will bring forward new opportunities that can help you achieve your goal. You may find that what you thought you wanted wasn't right for you after all, and this new opportunity will present fresh ideas on a way forward.

1 Ensure that you are in a calm mood. Sip water. Breathe in and out in a gentle, conscious, yet unforced way.

2 Once you have reached a feeling of calm, close your eyes and state your intention to be able to attract the opportunities that are right for you. You can be specific if you require an opportunity in a particular area, for example, a buyer for your house or a home to rent abroad.

3 Keeping your eyes closed, place your hands, one over the other, at your belly button with the palm of the hand closest to your body resting gently on your stomach.

4 As you breathe in and out, imagine that there is a force field of light that is emanating from your body on the in breath and contracting toward your body on the out breath. Then rest your hands, palms up, on your lap.

5 Now visualize the force field of light around you growing brighter and larger. Imagine that it is pulsing with a pure attractive energy. This is now magnetized and aligned to all those opportunities that are the very best for you.

6 Say out loud: "I trust the Universe to bring me what I need, in a loving manner. Thank you."

7 Turn your palms downward on your lap and rub them against your thighs. Gently open your eyes when you are ready.

8 Keep an eye out for anything that looks like it might be the opportunity you requested. It is not enough to simply do a meditation; you must also take actions in the mundane everyday world.

Further Reading

Advanced Studies of the Human Aura: How to Charge Your Energy Field with Light and Spiritual Radiance by David Christopher Lewis (Meru Pr, 2013)

Auras and How to Read Them by Sarah Bartlett (Collins and Brown, 2000)

Black Holes and Energy Pirates by Jesse Reeder (Gateway, 2001)

Chakras by Julian Flanders (Arcturus, 2020)

Energy Secrets by Alla Svirinskaya (Hay House, 2005)

How to Read the Aura by W.E. Butler (Thorsons, 1979)

Intermediate Studies of the Human Aura by Djwal Kul (Summit University Press, 1976)

Man Visible and Invisible by C.W. Leadbeater (1903)

Own Your Energy by Alla Svirinskaya (Hay House, 2019)

Studies of the Human Aura by Kuthumi (Summit University Press, 1976)

The Etheric Body of Man by Laurence J. Bendit & Phoebe D. Bendit (Quest, 1990)

The Etheric Double by Arthur E. Powell (Theosophical Publishing House, 1925)

The Inner Life by C.W. Leadbeater (1910)

The Science of the Aura by S.G.J. Ouseley (L.N. Fowler & Co, 1949)

Understanding Auras by Joseph Ostrom (HarperCollins, 1987)

Working with Auras by Jane Struthers (Godsfield Press, 2006)

Your Electro-Vibratory Body by Victor R. Beasley (University of the Trees Press, 1975)

FURTHER READING

ONLINE RESOURCES

College of Psychic Studies: collegeofpsychicstudies.co.uk

The Theosophical Society: theosophicalsociety.org.uk

Aloha International: huna.org

Index

A
Advaita Vedanta 17
alternate-nostril breathing 21, 43, 72–73
ancestors 7, 54
atman 17, 20
axis mundi 68

B
barefoot 30
body massage 29
brahman 16–17
Brahmavidya, Swami 67
Buddha 13, 23
Butler, W.E. 13

C
Cayce, Edgar 111
chakras, 12, 21, 36–63
    hand 88–89
    seven-chakra system 38–53
        Muladhara root chakra 40–41
        Svadhisthana sacral chakra 42–43
        Manipura solar plexus chakra 44–45
        Anahata heart chakra 46–47
        Visuddha throat chakra 48–49
        Ajna third eye chakra 50–51
        Sahasrara crown chakra 52
    Sufi chakra system 56–63
        Point of mantle 63
        Point of mystery 61
        Point of soul 60
        Point of the carnal self 58
        Point of the heart 59
        Point of veiled 62
chanting 8, 22, 28, 39, 41, 43, 44, 49, 57, 60
Christ 13
colors 6, 33, 39, 54–55, 57, 99, 133
cord-cutting 119

D
dance 7, 42, 57, 58
dervishes 8
devotee(s) 7, 8
dhamal 8, 58, 60
divine energy 7, 8, 59

E
energy
    body 6–8, 12–13, 15, 17, 24–25, 45,
    52, 54, 63, 97, 114, 119, 127, 131
    vampires 116–117

G
gazing 60, 69
    See also sagale-naseer
Gibran, Kahlil 8
God 58
    99 names of, 8
goddess 12
gods 7

H
halos 13
henna 90–91
herbs 26
Hills, Christopher 12
Hinduism 12
Huna 14–15

I
Indian subcontinent 8, 12
invisible energies 6, 137

INDEX

K
Kabuko the Djinn 6
King, Serge Kahili 14, 15
Kilner, Dr W.J. 33
    Screens 33–34
Kirlian, Semyon Davidovich & Valentina 32
    photography 32–33
koshas 16–25
    Anandamaya kosha 16, 24
    Annamaya kosha 16, 20
    Manomaya kosha 16, 22
    Pranamaya kosha 16, 21
    Vijnanamaya kosha 16, 23

L
lataifa 57–63
Leadbeater, Charles Webster 12

M
manifestation 7
meditation 8, 12, 17, 22–24, 31, 47, 52, 59, 60, 69, 105, 119, 120, 124–155
music 6–7, 57

N
Naaf, the 44, 67–69
navel 42, 67–69, 76, 83
    navel-gazing 69

O
oils 29–30, 51

P
Powell, Arthur E. 34

R
Rumi 49

S
sacred space 96–97

sagale-naseer 60
salt baths 27
Shah Madhu Lal Hussain 7
sheath, energy 12, 17, 20–21
    See also koshas
shrines 8
smudging 25–26
spirits 7
stone circles 102–103
Sufi 7, 8, 49, 54
chakras 57–63
Sufism 8,
Svirinskaya, Alla 74, 110

T
tea 108
theosophy 12–13
thought-forms 120
trance dance 7, 8, 57, 58
    See also Dhamal

V
Virgin Mary 13

W
water 15, 27–28, 104, 127, 130, 135, 137, 141, 144, 147, 150, 153,
Weil, Dr Andrew 30

Y
yoga 50, 70, 74–87
    Child's Pose 84–85
    Cobra Pose 82–83
    Corpse Pose 86–87
    Mountain Pose 76–77
    Tree Pose 78–79
    Warrior Pose 80–81